GREAT
★ POTATO ★
RECIPES
FROM AROUND THE WORLD

Mara Reid Rogers ★ Photography by Mark Hill

CASSELL

A RUNNING HEADS BOOK

Copyright © 1992 by Running Heads Incorporated.
Photographs © 1992 by Mark Hill.

First published in U.K. by Cassell Publishers 1992.
Cassell Publishers Limited
Villiers House
41/47 Strand
London WC2N 5JE

GREAT POTATO RECIPES FROM
AROUND THE WORLD
was conceived and produced by
Running Heads Incorporated
55 West 21 Street
New York, New York 10010

Editor: Rose K. Phillips
Managing Editor: Jill Hamilton
Production Manager: Peter J. McCulloch

1 3 5 7 9 10 8 6 4 2

British Library Cataloguing in Publication Data is available for this
title.

ISBN 0 304 34143 6

Typeset by Trufont Typographers, Inc.
Colour separations by Hong Kong Scanner Craft Company, Ltd.
Printed and bound in Singapore by Tien Wah Press (Pte.) Ltd.

DEDICATION

Often I am reminded of the message in Marcia Brown's folktale 'The Stone Soup'. The story is about three hungry soldiers who ask some villagers for food. The people refuse to share their food, each having a good reason. But the knowing and clever soldiers decide to make 'stone soup'. The villagers, very curious and anxious to glean the recipe, provide them with what they ask for, beginning with a 'large iron pot', 'many buckets of water' and 'three round, smooth stones'. The story unfolds with the soldiers hinting at other ingredients that would make the soup taste even better (yes, potatoes were amongst them!); strangely enough, the villagers suddenly found food to share. 'A rich man's soup — and all from a few stones. It seemed like magic!'

ACKNOWLEDGEMENTS

Many thanks to the entire crew at Running Heads, particularly Marta Hallett and Fran Obeid for sharing 'the idea', and Rose Phillips for keeping it alive and well. Also to Chris Fagg of Cassell and Norma MacMillan.

And to Mark, talented photographer and 'superhusband,' my boundless thanks for his participation in this international pursuit of the spud.

★CONTENTS★

2
Baked and Roasted
38

Potato and Rosemary Tuiles ★ Potato Pirog ★ Spud Burgers Deluxe ★ Sweet Potato Vine Biscuits ★ Individual Potato Moussakas ★ Bourbon-Glazed Sweet Potato and Banana Pone ★ Shepherd's Pie with Orange Potato Topping ★ Dilled Buttermilk Potato Bread ★ Potato Pizza with Caramelised Shallots ★ Chorizo and Potato Quesadillas ★ Sweet Potato Silver Dollars ★ Malarabia ★ Potato Chocolate Bread with Orange Chocolate Butter ★ Sweet Potato Custard ★ Down-Under Roadside Pasties ★ Flourless Honey Pecan Potato Torte ★ Potato and Cheese Strudel with Glacé Fruit ★ Chocolate Pecan Tart with Sweet Potato Crust

Introduction
6

1
Boiled and Steamed
10

Potato Salads from Around the World ★ Greek-Style Potato Salad ★ Cuban-Style Potato Salad ★ Coconut-Scented Potato and Lobster Bisque ★ Potato and Spinach Gnocchi with Carrot-Nutmeg Sauce ★ Steak and Potato Salad with Capers ★ Potato and Chestnut Stuffing with Sage ★ Pine Kernel and Potato Ravioli with Pumpkin Sauce ★ Potato and Asparagus Frittata ★ Potato and Caraway Scones ★ Himmel und Erde ★ Sweet Potato Ice Cream ★ Dessert Dumplings with Prune Butter Filling and Apricot Sauce

3
Mashed, Scalloped, and Au Gratin

Mashed Potato Dishes From Around the World ★ Chinese-Style Mashed Potatoes ★ Swiss-Style Mashed Potatoes ★ Potato, Tomato and Artichoke Gratin on Bed of Wild Rice ★ Potato and Bacon-Stuffed Cabbage Bundles ★ Iranian Style Cinnamon Scalloped Potatoes with Grated Turnip ★ Mashed Potato and Thyme Soup with Popcorn Croutons ★ Potato and Kasha Knishes ★ Shaker-Style Stewed Potatoes ★ Skordalia ★ Farmers' Potato and Onion Pudding ★ Peruvian-Style Stuffed Potato Balls ★ Individual Potato and Cheese Soufflés with Wild Mushrooms ★ Carrot and Potato Tea Cakes

4
Sautéed and Fried

Bubble and Squeak ★ Potato Curry ★ Latkes ★ Potatoes Paprikash ★ Game Chips or Crisps ★ Caramelised Potatoes ★ Chillied Batter-Fried Shoestring Potatoes ★ Hasselback Potatoes ★ Secret Ingredient Cookies ★ Blue Ribbon Sweet Potato Doughnuts ★ Sweet Potato Tempura with Dipping Sauce ★ Dum Aloo

INTRODUCTION

The potato is much more than a source of food. It has actually had an impact on worldwide social and economic events, thereby making its mark — or 'potato-print', so to speak — on history. Were I to characterise the potato, I would call it proud. And certainly, as you shall soon read, it has the right to be so. The white potato, as we know it now, has had a romantic but difficult history: its genesis was one of many transformations. It started as a simple tuber, became an esteemed symbol of prosperity, and later was reduced to being a lowly pauper. Luckily, though it took many lifetimes, the potato is now considered king of the vegetables and rightly so.

Potatoes have existed since at least 3000 B.C. They were domesticated by the now legendary Incas of South America. The white potato began as a wild root ball deep in the ground of the Andes Mountains in Peru. The potato had proven itself an extremely hardy and tolerant tuber; the Incas grew potatoes at an altitude of 2400 metres above where maize could prosper.

Imagine the Incas gathering potatoes amidst the cold, wind-whipped mountains. And what a harvest it was! They had hundreds of varieties of wild potatoes, ranging in size from that of a grape to a grapefruit. Their potatoes also came in many shapes and textures, and the panoply of colours from white to orange, pink to purple, blue, green, brown and black. The Incas dedicated ceremonies to the potato and it became an object of worship and much pride. They felt the humble potato was a gift bestowed upon them. It was a secret, though, that they could not hold forever. After much trial and tribulation the potato would become — many, many years later — a gift to the entire world.

Legend has it that in the sixteenth century Spanish explorers led by Pizarro in search of treasure plundered the Incas' silver mine and happened upon their potatoes — the true treasure! The potato, consequently, sailed back to Spain amongst the chests of other riches. However, from there the pages of the potato's scrapbook diverge. The common belief is that the English word 'potato' evolved from *batata*, the word for the sweet potato amongst the Arawak Indians of the Caribbean Islands. The sweet potato, along with the yam — two delicious types that are unrelated to each other or the white potato — may also have first been brought to Europe by the Spaniards.

There are many theories and even more speculation as to how the true potato travelled from Spain to the rest of the world —

in particular, to European and North American dinner tables. One of the most popular beliefs is that the potato cargo of the Spanish sailors was later cultivated throughout the world's gardens simply because of its decorative flowers; the edible virtues were realised afterwards.

Though we do know that through commerce the potato made its way across Europe and to the British Isles, there are numerous tales as to how it happened. It is suggested that in 1586, potatoes were transported on the ships of Sir Francis Drake to the Roanoke Island colony through something of a fluke. It seems that Drake had been doing battle with Spaniards who had established outposts in the Caribbean. After successful warring, he was ready to return to England, but first needed to stock up on provisions. He had heard that some of the British colonists on Roanoke were disgruntled and wanted to return home. Drake made a stop in Colombia for supplies — amongst them, potatoes. As he picked up the colonists, he left some of his cargo in North America. He transported the rest of the potatoes back to England, where they slowly gained popularity. It is thought that Sir Walter Raleigh was given some potatoes from this cargo, planted them on his estate in Ireland, and presented Queen Elizabeth with some choice specimens. Unfortunately her chef did not do the potato justice: he discarded the tubers but cooked the bitter leaves. Perhaps because

of errors in preparation such as this one, the spud's attributes remained largely unrealised in Europe from the sixteenth to the eighteenth centuries.

Europeans were reluctant to accept the 'lowly' potato because it was considered an evil and decadent food. They avoided the potato because it belonged to the nightshade plant family, and it was thought to closely resemble the poisonous European nightshade, known as the 'Devil's herb'. Another punitive mark was that the potato was not mentioned in the Bible, which made it suspect as a wholesome food.

There were also many superstitions about the potato, such as the belief that if a pregnant woman were to eat one, her baby would be born with an abnormally small head. Folk beliefs connected the potato to various physical maladies, amongst them leprosy and syphilis. The misconceptions were many, and the potato was in for a tough time.

The Irish, who were the first Europeans to grow potatoes as a staple carbohydrate, were devastated by the Potato Famine in the 1840s. At this time, the potato was the main source of food in Ireland. So when the potato blight caused huge crop losses, the six years of famine resulted in an estimated one million deaths. Needless to say, this event did not help the reputation of the potato.

Even though the potato played a part in many people's diet, the white potato still had few friends well into the nineteenth century. Yet throughout history, there were influential supporters of the potato, who believed in its culinary possibilities even when public opinion ran against it.

One of the potato's strongest proponents was Frederick William I, King of Prussia, who believed that the potato was the answer to hunger amongst his subjects. In about 1720, he threatened to cut off the ears and noses of anyone who refused to farm spuds. Most of the peasants ignored his decree, and when he issued it again in 1750 they continued to disobey. The story goes that in desperation he ate potatoes on his palace balcony for all the world to see; his subjects then reconsidered the spud and decided that if it were fit for a king, it must certainly be good enough for them.

Another spud supporter was the French pharmacist Antoine-Auguste Parmentier, who also believed that the potato could help put an end to widespread hunger. He urged King Louis XVI to grant him use of land near Paris to farm potatoes. After raising a healthy crop, he had the king station royal guards round the field, his motivation being to entice the local peasants into stealing the valuable crops. Parmentier had the guards withdraw one night so that the peasants could take the potatoes. Thus began the process of the dissemination of the potato throughout France. Parmentier is the namesake of many traditional French potato dishes, including a soup and an omelette. He 'marketed' the potato as a solution to France's intermittent famine. When the Academy of Besançon held a contest for the best 'study of food substances capable of reducing the calamities of famine', Parmentier was the winner because he touted the virtues of the potato so eloquently.

Stories abound of famous fêtes at which he entertained the elite as well as world-renowned political officials such as Benjamin Franklin with nothing to eat but potato-based dishes. At a court dinner which Parmentier 'catered', Marie Antoinette was said to have worn potato flowers in her hair!

It wasn't until about the mid-nineteenth century that the potato received some of the tremendous respect it deserved round the world. It was recognised that not only would the potato grow well under poor conditions, but that it matured quickly, produced abundantly, could be harvested after sixty days, and stored well. The potato lends itself to both commercial production and garden cultivation, so it could be grown by the farmer and the cottager. Since the potato grows underground it could survive the trampling of soldiers in a war and the worst of Mother Nature's tantrums. Perhaps most important, people finally realised that the potato was also filling and delicious: you could eat one and feel satisfied.

By the end of the nineteenth century, the plight of the potato had changed for the better; the fears were forgotten, our hero had emerged a victor! The potato was a part of daily life, and cookery books had a multitude of recipes using this nutritious tuber. The potato had arrived.

Today the potato is the most important vegetable crop in the world, and the third most important food crop. The power and popularity of the spud is well established. Potato consumption is very high in many countries, and the figures are escalating. There are many rediscovered varieties of potatoes that now exist but, although they are reminiscent of the first Andean potatoes and their rainbow of colours, the potato has been improved upon and has more flavour and better resistance to disease than in bygone centuries.

GREAT POTATO RECIPES FROM AROUND THE WORLD is a collection of recipes in which the potato is the star. The recipes I have created have been inspired by traditional ethnic potato and sweet potato preparations, or are evocative of a specific country and draw ingredients from its larder. I have added my own personal touch to each recipe in an effort to make a healthy and delicious dish. For instance, I have added celery seed to the Jewish-American *Latkes* (page 110) for flavour and to replace excess salt. Ground cumin is amongst the seasonings used in *Shepherd's Pie with Orange and Potato Topping* (page 52) — though it isn't a traditional British spice, it is quite delicious with lamb.

I have tried to bring you a wide range of recipes, not only in their international scope and flavours, but in their various cookery methods and the time it takes to prepare them. All of the recipes are easy; some are rustic and 'homey', others are elegant and appropriate for entertaining.

The potato is not only a nutritious, low-calorie vegetable that can be enjoyed year-round, it is also an extremely versatile ingredient that can be served up in many guises. As you'll see in these pages, the potato can take the form of a starter, side dish, condiment, main course, or even dessert!

My hope is that, after trying some of the recipes, not only will your tastebuds be thrilled, but you will be as impressed and enthralled with the potato as I am. I have fallen in love with the potato, for it is far more than just a flavour. Its impact on cooking is far-ranging, whether it adds moistness to a bread, sweetness to a cake, or texture and stability to a dressing or sauce.

This book is a celebration of the potato for its place in history and for the inspiration and sustenance it continues to give. Suffice it to say, the motive was simple: what better way to pay tribute to the potato than by writing a cookery book!

— Mara Reid Rogers

Boiled and Steamed

1

Salad:

900 g (2 lb) small new potatoes,
   unpeeled, halved crossways if
   large
1 medium red onion, very thinly
   sliced
1 medium yellow pepper, cored,
   seeded and thinly sliced
1 medium red or green pepper,
   cored, seeded and thinly
   sliced
175 g (6 oz) feta cheese, rinsed,
   patted dry and crumbled
2 ripe but firm medium
   tomatoes, seeded and cut
   into eighths
90 g (3 oz) Greek Kalamata
   olives or other brine-cured
   olives, rinsed, stoned and
   halved lengthways

Dressing:

Makes 250 ml (8 fl oz)

125 ml (4 fl oz) fresh lemon
   juice
125 ml (4 fl oz) olive oil
2 cloves garlic, crushed
1½ tablespoons finely chopped
   fresh mint
1 tablespoon finely chopped
   fresh oregano
Salt and freshly ground pepper
   to taste
Anchovy fillets, rinsed and
   patted dry, to garnish
   (optional)

1. To prepare the salad: place the potatoes directly on a rack or in a steamer basket in a large saucepan over 5 cm (2 in) of boiling water (the water level should not touch the bottom of the rack). Cover the saucepan and steam for 10 to 15 minutes (depending on the size of the potatoes), or until they are tender when the centre of the thickest potato is pierced with a fork. Discard the cooking water and drain the potatoes in a colander under cool running water. Allow to cool to room temperature.

2. Meanwhile, prepare the dressing: in a medium non-metallic bowl whisk together the lemon juice, olive oil, garlic, mint and oregano until well blended. Season with salt and pepper.

3. To assemble the salad: in a large non-metallic bowl toss together the potatoes and half of the dressing and leave the potatoes to cool completely.

4. Add the red onion, yellow and red pepper feta cheese, tomatoes and olives and the remaining dressing. Toss gently until well combined. Garnish with the anchovy fillets if using. Serve at room temperature or chilled.

GREEK-STYLE POTATO SALAD

(GREECE)

Serves 4 to 6

Salad:

5 medium firm-fleshed potatoes
   (page 133)
1 × 120 g (4 oz) jar or can
   chopped pimientos, drained
1 × 400 g (14 oz) can black or
   red kidney beans, drained
   and rinsed
1 ripe but-firm medium avocado

Dressing:
Makes 250 ml (8 fl oz)
4 tablespoons white wine
   vinegar
3 tablespoons fresh lime juice
125 ml (4 fl oz) sunflower or
   vegetable oil
2 cloves garlic, crushed
120 g (4 oz) red onion, finely
   chopped
½ teaspoon ground cumin
½ teaspoon chilli powder
¼ teaspoon ground saffron
   (optional)
Salt and freshly ground pepper
   to taste

(CUBA)

Serves 4

1. To prepare the salad: place the potatoes directly on a rack or in a steamer basket in a large saucepan over 5 cm (2 in) of boiling water. Cover the saucepan and steam for 10 to 25 minutes, until potatoes are tender. Drain in a colander under cold running water. Allow to cool.

2. Meanwhile, prepare the dressing: in a medium non-metallic bowl whisk together ingredients.

3. Peel potatoes and cut into 1 cm (½ in) slices, then cut with a geometric shape pastry cutter.

4. In a large non-metallic bowl toss the potatoes and one-third of the dressing.

5. Add the pimientos, black beans and another third of the dressing and toss gently until well combined.

6. Cut the avocado into 16 slices. Lay 4 avocado slices round each salad. Drizzle the remaining dressing.

★ OTHER INTERNATIONAL POTATO SALADS ★

★ English-Style: Combine cooked, sliced potatoes with watercress leaves and crumbled blue Stilton cheese. ★ Russian-Style: Combine cooked, sliced potatoes with thinly sliced cooked beet-root, soured cream, thinly sliced cucumber and finely chopped onions. ★ Scandinavian-Style: Combine cooked, sliced potatoes with finely chopped fresh dill and slices of smoked salmon.

CUBAN-STYLE POTATO SALAD

1 litre (1¾ pints) fish stock

2 stalks fresh lemon grass, thinly
   sliced and smashed with the
   back of a heavy frying pan,
   or 1 × 7.5 cm (3 in) strip
   fresh lemon zest

3 kaffir lime leaves (available at
   a shop specialising in Thai
   food) or 1 × 7.5 cm (3 in)
   strip of fresh lime zest

Good pinch cayenne pepper

3 medium firm-fleshed potatoes
   (page 132), cooked, peeled
   and cut into 1 cm (½ in) dice

350 g (12 oz) cooked lobster
   meat, thawed if frozen, cut
   into 2.5 cm (1 in) julienne

3 spring onions, including
   7.5 cm (3 in) of green part,
   thinly sliced, to garnish

4 tablespoons canned
   unsweetened coconut milk, not
   canned cream of coconut

1. In a non-metallic heavy-based saucepan over medium high heat, combine the fish stock, lemon grass, lime leaves and cayenne pepper and bring to the boil. Strain, discarding the lemon grass and lime leaves (or lemon zest and lime zest), and return the stock to the saucepan over low heat.

2. Stir the potatoes, lobster and white part of the spring onions into the stock and simmer for 5 to 7 minutes, stirring often, just until the potatoes are heated through. Remove the saucepan from the heat and pour the mixture into a large bowl. Stir 125 ml (4 fl oz) of the hot mixture into the coconut milk in a small bowl, then stir this mixture back into the large bowl until well blended. Sprinkle with green part of spring onions. Serve at once.

> "A man went out in his garden one day to dig some potatoes and sell them for pay. As he started to dig, one of them said, 'Well who in the world got you out of bed? For all this time you've let the weeds grow. Now here you come with your shovel and hoe. No thanks to you that at last I'm grown. Go away and leave me alone!' . . . Said the farmer, 'I heard my potato say, "Leave me alone! Go away!" And my dog stopped chewing on this bone and said, "You leave that potato alone!"'"
> —*Ennis Rees*, Potato Talk, *1969*

COCONUT-SCENTED POTATO AND LOBSTER BISQUE

(THAILAND)

Serves 4, about 300 ml

(½ pint) per serving

Gnocchi:

5 medium floury potatoes,
  peeled

3 cloves garlic, halved
  lengthways

215 g (7½ oz) unbleached plain
  flour, plus more to knead
  dough

60 g (2 oz) Parmesan cheese,
  freshly grated

½ teaspoon salt

½ teaspoon freshly ground
  white pepper

60 g (2 oz) cooked fresh or
  thawed frozen spinach,
  drained, finely chopped and
  squeezed dry

Good pinch freshly grated
  nutmeg

Butter to grease baking dish

Sauce:

Makes about 350 ml (12 fl oz)

250 ml (8 fl oz) fresh or canned
  carrot juice, at room
  temperature

Good pinch freshly grated
  nutmeg

125 ml (4 fl oz) milk, at room
  temperature

Salt and freshly ground white
  pepper to taste

4 tablespoons Parmesan cheese
  shavings, to garnish
  (optional)

POTATO AND SPINACH GNOCCHI WITH CARROT-NUTMEG SAUCE

(ITALY)

Serves 4, about
15 gnocchi each

1. To prepare the gnocchi: place the potatoes directly on a rack or in a steamer basket in a large saucepan over 5 cm (2 in) of boiling water (the water level should not touch the bottom of the rack or basket). Add the halved garlic cloves to the water, cover the saucepan and steam the potatoes for 30 to 40 minutes, or until they are tender when the thickest part of a potato is pierced with a fork. Drain the potatoes in a colander, discarding the cooking water and garlic.

2. When the potatoes are cool enough to handle, but still warm, mash them with a potato ricer or masher or in a food mill until smooth. (*Note:* Do not use a food processor or the potatoes will become too gluey.)

3. On a lightly floured work surface make 2 equal mounds with the flour and sprinkle each with half of the Parmesan cheese, salt and white pepper. In the centre of each mound form a well. Place half of the mashed potatoes in each well. Put the dry cooked spinach and the nutmeg in the centre of only one of the wells. Gradually draw the flour into the first well, little by little, gently mixing it with the potatoes until the mixture is well blended. Gradually draw the flour into the potato and spinach, making a dough. You should now have two separate masses of dough, one plain potato, one spinach and potato. The dough should be slightly sticky.

4. Working quickly, on a lightly floured work surface knead each type of dough about 20 turns or until smooth. Refrigerate until ready to use. (The recipe can be made up to this point 1 day ahead. Wrap and refrigerate each type of dough separately.)

5. On a lightly floured work surface, break off several pieces of plain potato dough and, using your palms, roll each of the pieces into a 2.5 cm (1 in) thick rope. Slice each rope into 5 mm (¼ in) wide pieces, and roll each piece into a ball. Repeat this entire process with the spinach and potato dough. Carefully transfer the pieces to a baking sheet and cover lightly with cling film.

6. To shape the gnocchi: lightly dust your fingertips with flour. Using the side of a box grater with the small, raised perforations, gently roll a piece of plain dough from the top of the grater round in a 'c' shaped motion, pushing your thumb into the centre of the dough ball as you do so. You should now have a concave dumpling with a raised dot pattern. (*Note*: The centre of each dumpling should be about the same thickness as the exterior, so that the dumplings cook evenly.) If the dough sticks to the grater, lightly dust the grater with flour. If the dough is too sticky to work with, gently blend some more flour into the dough. Repeat with the remaining plain potato dough, returning each dumpling to the baking sheet when done. Then repeat the process with the spinach and potato dough. When all the gnocchi have been shaped, lightly re-cover them with

★ POTATO SCIENCE ★
New Frontiers

As of 1991, the USDA (US Department of Agriculture) is in the process of trying to create high-quality potatoes called 'superspuds', by using 'microtubers' (laboratory-reared potatoes that have been genetically engineered).

Alan Reed of Reed's Dairy Farm in the state of Idaho has created Spudscream, an all-natural ice cream that contains 40 percent fewer calories than his regular ice cream. 'Al & Reed's Sugar Free Ice Cream' is made with cream, milk, apple sweetener and potato flakes and comes in a variety of flavours: chocolate, strawberry, raspberry, banana-berry, chocolate and almond, butter pecan and vanilla.

★ Scientists at the Argonne National Laboratory in the state of Illinois are developing a process to convert potato starch from potato peelings into bio- and photodegradable plastics.

★ The Ukrainian Academy of Sciences has carried out tests on a generator that uses potatoes as an electricity source. The scientists claim that a potato can produce electricity for almost a month.

★ JR Simplot of Idaho has produced ethanol from potatoes, which enhances octane and lowers the pollution level of gasoline. His scientists have also figured out a way to turn the potato sludge from making the ethanol into thrifty fish food.

★ The US Department of Agriculture has created "Super Slurper," a powder made from potatoes that is able to absorb upon contact thousands of times its weight of liquid.

the cling film and reserve at room temperature until you are ready to cook them.

7. Into a very large pan of boiling water drop a single layer of plain potato gnocchi (about 10 to 12 per batch) at a time. Boil for about 8 to 10 minutes, stirring gently once or twice to prevent the gnocchi from sticking to one another or the bottom of the pan, or until they float to the surface. Using a slotted spoon, remove the batch of gnocchi, drain well and transfer to a lightly buttered large shallow baking dish. Do not layer the gnocchi or let them touch each other. Repeat the process with the remaining plain potato gnocchi, then cook the spinach and potato gnocchi in the same manner, adding each batch to the baking dish as they are done.

8. Lightly cover the dish with foil and keep warm in a very low oven until ready to serve.

9. Meanwhile, prepare the sauce: in a medium non-metallic bowl whisk together the carrot juice, nutmeg and milk until well blended. (*Note:* The sauce will have the consistency of a dressing.) Season to taste with salt and pepper.

10. To serve, divide the gnocchi among 4 plates (be sure to include both the plain potato and the potato and spinach gnocchi on each plate), drizzle with the sauce (the heat of the gnocchi will warm the sauce) and garnish with the Parmesan shavings if using. Serve at once.

TEAK AND POTATO SALAD WITH CAPERS

(UNITED STATES)

Serves 6

*900 g (2 lb) small red and
white new potatoes, unpeeled
and halved if large*

*125 ml (4 fl oz) malt vinegar or
red wine vinegar*

1 tablespoon caster sugar

*4 tablespoons finely chopped
fresh basil, plus 2 whole
leaves, to garnish*

*2 tablespoons finely chopped
fresh oregano or 2 teaspoons
dried, crumbled*

½ teaspoon salt

*½ teaspoon freshly ground
pepper*

250 ml (8 fl oz) olive oil

*45 g (1½ oz) drained capers,
rinsed*

*1 × 450 g (1 lb) sirloin or rump
steak, grilled until cooked to
taste, cut into 5 mm (¼ in)
thick slices*

*4 hard-boiled eggs, thinly sliced,
to garnish*

1. Place the potatoes directly on a rack or in a steamer basket in a large saucepan over 5 cm (2 in) of boiling water (the water level should not touch the bottom of the rack). Cover the saucepan and steam for 10 to 25 minutes (depending on the size of the potatoes) or until tender. Discard the cooking water, and drain the potatoes in a colander under cold running water.

2. In a medium non-metallic bowl whisk together the vinegar, sugar, basil, oregano, salt and pepper until well blended. Gradually pour in the olive oil in a slow steady stream, whisking until the oil is completely incorporated and emulsified. Adjust seasoning to taste.

3. In a large non-metallic bowl gently toss together the potatoes, the dressing and capers.

4. To serve, mound the salad in the centre of a platter and surround with overlapping steak slices. Arrange an overlapping ring of egg slices round the edge of the platter round the steak. Decoratively arrange the whole basil leaves on the potato salad and serve.

> *"Be eating one potato, peeling a second, have a third in your fist, and your eye on a fourth."*
>
> *—Advice of an old man to a young man at the dinner table (an old Irish saying)*

5 medium firm-fleshed potatoes,
   peeled
1 medium onion, finely chopped
6 slices white bread, crusts
   removed and cut into 1 cm
   (½ in) dice
4 stalks celery, finely chopped,
   leaves included
350 g (12 oz) red or green
   seedless grapes, washed
   thoroughly, dried and halved
   lengthways
1 × 350 g (12 oz) can peeled
   whole chestnuts (brine-
   packed), drained, rinsed and
   finely chopped
30 g (1 oz) unsalted butter,
   melted
2 teaspoons finely chopped fresh
   sage or 1 teaspoon ground
   sage
½ teaspoon salt
1 teaspoon freshly ground
   pepper
250 ml (8 fl oz) home-made
   beef stock

1. Place the potatoes directly on a rack or in a steamer basket in a large saucepan over 5 cm (2 in) of boiling water (the water level should not touch the bottom of the rack). Cover the saucepan and steam the potatoes for 30 to 40 minutes or until they are tender when the thickest part is pierced with a fork. Drain the potatoes in a colander, discarding the cooking water. When the potatoes are cool enough to handle, cut them into 1 cm (½ in) dice and reserve.

2. In a large bowl combine the onion, bread, celery, grapes, chestnuts, melted butter, sage, salt and pepper. Then add the reserved potatoes and stock and, using your hands, gently toss together (so as not to break the potatoes) until well blended. Allow to cool completely before stuffing the poultry. Stuff poultry and roast as usual. Or bake the stuffing separately in an uncovered casserole until heated through and lightly browned. (*Note*: Do not store raw or cooked stuffing in cavity of poultry. After serving, transfer any stuffing remaining in the cavity to a container, cover and refrigerate for up to 2 days.)

> *"No man can be wise on an empty stomach."*
> —George Eliot

Makes enough to fill the cavity of a 3.6 to 4.5 kg (8 to 10 lb) duck, goose, chicken or turkey

POTATO AND CHESTNUT STUFFING WITH SAGE

(UNITED STATES)

Pasta:

*Makes 350 g (12 oz) (Or substitute
2 sheets, total of 350 g (12 oz) of
fresh egg pasta dough.)*

*300 g (10 oz) plain flour, plus
more if needed*

3 size-3 eggs, lightly beaten

*1 size-3 egg, lightly beaten, to
seal*

Filling:

*1 teaspoon olive oil or sunflower
oil*

45 g (1½ oz) pine kernels

*325 g (11 oz) smoothly mashed
potatoes (page 139)*

1 size-3 egg, lightly beaten

2 cloves garlic, crushed

*1 tablespoon finely chopped
fresh marjoram or oregano*

*2 tablespoons finely chopped
fresh chives*

*Salt and freshly ground pepper
to taste*

PINE KERNEL AND POTATO RAVIOLI WITH PUMPKIN SAUCE

(ITALY)

*Serves 4,
6 ravioli per serving*

1. To prepare the pasta: sift the flour into a mound on a work surface and make a well in the centre. Pour the 3 beaten eggs into the well. Using your fingertips or a fork, mix the flour and eggs together until the dough begins to form a rough mass. If the dough is too sticky to handle, add some more flour. Using a pastry scraper scrape the work surface, preventing the dough from spreading.

2. Gather the dough into a ball and knead for about 5 minutes or until the dough is smooth and satiny, adding a little flour if needed. Divide the dough into 2 equal parts and form each into a flat disc. Wrap each disc tightly in cling film, and refrigerate for 1 hour. (The pasta dough can be refrigerated up to 1 day. Return to room temperature, but keep wrapped until proceeding with the recipe.)

3. To prepare the filling: in a small heavy frying pan over medium low heat, heat the olive oil. Add the pine kernels and cook, stirring constantly, for about 3 to 4 minutes or until evenly toasted a light golden brown. (Be careful not to overcook or the pine kernels will be bitter.) Immediately transfer to kitchen paper to drain.

4. In a medium bowl combine the mashed potatoes, egg, garlic, marjoram and chives and mix until well blended. Season with salt and pepper and gently stir in half of the pine kernels, reserving the remainder for garnish. Cover and refrigerate until ready to use.

5. To prepare the sauce: force the pumpkin purée through a food mill fitted with a fine blade set over a small heavy saucepan until smooth. Whisk in the stock and olive oil, and season with salt and pepper to taste. Reserve at room temperature until ready to serve. (The sauce can be prepared up to 1 day ahead. Cover and refrigerate. Bring to room temperature before serving.)

6. To assemble the ravioli: set the rollers of a manual pasta machine to the most open position. Feed the first disc through the machine while cranking. Fold the dough in half lengthways and repeat. Repeat this process, folding the dough in half widthways. Continue until the dough is smooth and elastic. Wrap the first sheet in cling film and repeat with the second disc.

7. Beginning with the widest setting, roll out the first pasta sheet, once through each setting, down to the second to the thinnest setting. Trim to two 15 × 38 cm (6 × 15 in) rectangles. Cover with greaseproof paper and then damp kitchen paper, roll up in cling film and refrigerate. Repeat with the second pasta sheet.

8. Brush one rectangle with one-quarter of the beaten egg. Place 1 heaping teaspoon of the filling on the pasta, placing the filling in 2 rows of 6 mounds, 2.5 cm (1 in) apart and 2.5 cm (1 in) from each edge of the rectangle. Lightly brush the second rectangle of pasta with egg and lay it egg side down over filling. Press the sheets together to seal the ravioli. You will have 12 ravioli. Repeat the process with the second set of pasta rectangles.

9. Using a fluted pastry wheel, pastry cutter or knife, cut 5.5 cm (2¼ in) wide circles or squares. Transfer to a baking sheet lightly dusted with flour and reserve. Repeat with second set of sheets and filling.

10. In a very large heavy pan over high heat, bring 5 litres (8 pints) of water to the boil. Place the saucepan with pumpkin sauce over low heat until ready to serve.

11. Drop the ravioli into the boiling water and stir once gently. Bring to the boil again and boil for 4 to 6 minutes. Drain; divide ravioli, sauce and pine kernels among 4 plates.

Sauce:
Makes 250 ml (8 fl oz) (Or substitute 250 ml (8 fl oz) home-made tomato sauce.)
350 g (12 oz) puréed cooked fresh pumpkin
4 tablespoons chicken stock, preferably home-made

1 teaspoon olive oil, preferably extra virgin
Salt and freshly ground white pepper to taste

POTATO AND ASPARAGUS FRITTATA

(ITALY)

Serves 2

Filling:

1 tablespoon olive oil, plus more
    if needed
2 cloves garlic, crushed
1 small onion, coarsely chopped
120 g (4 oz) asparagus spears,
    steamed until just tender and
    cut lengthways into 2.5 cm
    (1 in) pieces
45 g (1½ oz) red pepper, finely
    chopped
45 g (1½ oz) brine-cured olives,
    preferably Greek Kalamata,
    stoned and halved lengthways
150 g (5 oz) firm-fleshed
    potatoes (page 133), cooked
    and thinly sliced
1½ teaspoons finely chopped
    fresh marjoram or 1 teaspoon
    dried, crumbled

Frittata:

4 size-3 eggs
Salt and freshly ground pepper
    to taste
3 tablespoons grated mozzarella

1. To prepare the filling: in a 25 cm (10 in) ovenproof frying pan over low heat, combine the olive oil, garlic and onion. Cook, stirring frequently, for 2 or 3 minutes, or until the onion has softened. Add the asparagus, red pepper, olives, potatoes and marjoram, with more olive oil as needed to coat the vegetables. Raise the heat to high and sauté the vegetables, stirring frequently, for about 3 minutes, or until the asparagus is fully tender. Remove the pan from the heat, cover and set aside at room temperature until ready to use.

2. Preheat the oven to 170°C (325°F or gas 3).

3. To prepare the frittata: in a medium bowl whisk together the eggs, 1 tablespoon water and a pinch of salt until well blended. Add the mozzarella and whisk until combined. Pour the egg mixture evenly over the vegetables in the pan.

4. Bake, uncovered, for 15 to 20 minutes or just until the eggs are set but not browned. Season with salt and pepper. Loosen the omelet with a palette knife and slide on to a warmed serving platter. Cut into wedges and serve at once.

POTATO AND CARAWAY SCONES

(ENGLAND)

Makes 12 scones

150 g (5 oz) plain flour
60 g (2 oz) Parmesan cheese,
    freshly grated
2 teaspoons baking powder
1 teaspoon dry mustard
½ teaspoon salt
¼ teaspoon freshly ground black
    pepper
60 g (2 oz) unsalted butter,
    diced and chilled
2 tablespoons olive oil,
    preferably extra virgin
1 size-3 egg, lightly beaten
2 cloves garlic, crushed
1 tablespoon caraway seeds
4 tablespoons skimmed milk
300 g (10 oz) firm-fleshed
    potatoes (page 132), cooked
    and cut into 5 mm (¼ in)
    dice
Low-fat soft cheese, to serve

1. Preheat the oven to 200°C (400°F or gas 6).

2. In a large mixing bowl combine the flour, Parmesan, baking powder, dry mustard, salt and pepper. With your fingertips, rub the cold butter into the flour mixture until it resembles coarse crumbs. Stir in the olive oil, egg, garlic, caraway seeds and milk until just blended. Gently fold in the diced potatoes to distribute evenly throughout the mixture, trying not to 'mash' the potatoes.

3. Drop well-rounded tablespoonfuls of the mixture on to an ungreased baking sheet about 2.5 cm (1 in) apart. Bake for 12 to 15 minutes, or until the edges are lightly golden. Serve warm with soft cheese for tea or to accompany soup.

★ SPUD STYLE OR POTATO ARTIFACTS ★

*A brief list of items that are either
in the shape of a potato or have
pictures of spuds on them:*

Postcards, burlap potato sacks (some converted to clothing), potato harvesting basket, souvenirs, cookie jars, toys such as Mr. Potato Head®, chinaware, pens, pencils, bookends, barrettes, buttons, jewelry, potato-based paint, postage stamps, potholders, candy, wallpaper, puzzles, placemats, napkins, stickers, hand lotion, stained-glass windows, make-up colors, shoes, Halloween potato costumes, stationery, shoes, furniture, and the list goes on . . .

5 medium tart dessert apples,
  preferably red-skinned,
  1 peeled and cut into 1 cm
  (½ in) dice
1 tablespoon fresh lemon juice
1 medium firm-fleshed potato,
  peeled and cut into 5 mm
  (¼ in) dice
Salt and freshly ground pepper
  to taste
4 thin rashers streaky bacon,
  rinded and coarsely chopped
1 medium onion, thinly sliced
  and separated into rings
Sunflower oil or vegetable oil to
  grease
1 teaspoon Calvados or cider
  vinegar

This Westphalian dish is composed of dense, unctuous potatoes—'earth'—and light, fluffy apples—'heaven'—hence its romantic name, which means heaven and earth.

1. Cut the top 1 cm (½ in) from the stalk end of each whole apple; set these 'lids' aside. Hollow out the bases using a spoon to make containers with 5 mm (¼ in) thick walls. Rub the inside of each apple container with lemon juice to prevent discoloration.

2. In a large, heavy-based saucepan over medium high heat, combine the diced apple, potato and 5 tablespoons water and bring to the boil. Reduce the heat to low and cover the saucepan tightly. Simmer, stirring once, for 15 minutes or until the potatoes are tender but not falling apart. Season with salt and pepper.

3. In a large heavy frying pan over medium high heat, fry the bacon for 6 minutes or until browned and crisp. Using a slotted spoon, transfer the bacon to kitchen paper to drain. Carefully pour off all but 1 tablespoon of the bacon fat and return the pan with the fat to medium heat. Add the onion rings. Cook, stirring often, for 5 to 7 minutes or until the rings are golden brown.

4. Preheat the oven to 200°C (400°F or gas 6). Lightly grease the bottom of a 23 cm (9 in) square baking dish with sunflower oil. Rub the outside of the 4 apple lids and containers with a little sunflower oil and place the apple containers in the baking dish so that they stand upright.

5. Stir the bacon and onion rings along with the Calvados into the apple and potato mixture until well blended. Divide the mixture among the apples, firmly packing it down into each container. Replace the apple lids.

6. Bake for 15 to 20 minutes or until the apples are heated through. Serve hot. *Himmel und Erde* is a perfect side dish to baked ham, country sausages or pork.

IMMEL UND ERDE   (GERMANY)

Serves 4

S WEET POTATO ICE CREAM

(JAPAN)

Makes 750 ml (1¼ pints)

400 ml (14 fl oz) milk
300 ml (½ pint) heavy cream
100 g (3½ oz) caster sugar
2 tablespoons grated peeled
  fresh root ginger or 1 table-
  spoon ground ginger
½ teaspoon ground cinnamon
½ teaspoon freshly grated
  nutmeg
4 size-3 egg yolks, at room
  temperature
250 g (9 oz) smoothly mashed
  yellow or orange fleshed
  sweet potatoes (page 139)
1 teaspoon vanilla essence
Crisp biscuits, preferably home-
  made, to serve (optional)

1. In a large heavy-based saucepan over low heat, combine the milk, cream, sugar, ginger, cinnamon and nutmeg. Cook for about 5 or 6 minutes, stirring often, or until the sugar dissolves and the mixture is heated through. Do not allow the mixture to boil. Allow to cool to room temperature.

2. In a heatproof medium bowl beat together the egg yolks and cooled milk mixture until well blended. Set the bowl over a pan of barely simmering water and cook for 15 to 20 minutes, stirring constantly in a figure of 8 motion, until the mixture has thickened and coats the back of the spoon. Do not allow the mixture to get too hot or boil, or the egg yolks will cook too much.

*"Here's taters hot, my
little chaps
Now just lay out a
copper,
I'm known up and
down the Strand,
You won't find any
hotter."*

—*The cry of a London
Potato Johnny during
the Victorian Age*

3. Remove the bowl from over the pan of hot water and stir in the mashed sweet potatoes a little at a time, until well blended. Using a fine-mesh sieve, sieve the custard into a large bowl, forcing the mashed sweet potatoes through with a wooden spoon but leaving any fibrous material behind.

4. Stir the vanilla essence into the custard mixture and allow to cool to room temperature, stirring occasionally as it cools. (This recipe can be made up to this point 1 day ahead. Allow to cool, cover and refrigerate.)

5. Freeze in an ice-cream maker according to the manufacturer's directions. To serve, scoop out and divide among bowls. Serve with biscuits if desired. To store: can be frozen for up to 4 days only (to assure maximum freshness).

ESSERT DUMPLINGS WITH PRUNE BUTTER FILLING AND APRICOT SAUCE

1. To prepare the dumplings: in a medium bowl mix together the mashed potatoes, egg yolks, salt and cloves until well blended. Then using your fingers, blend in the flour until a smooth dough is formed. (*Note*: The dough will be sticky.) Remove the dough from the bowl, form into a flat disc, wrap and refrigerate for 30 minutes.

2. To prepare the apricot sauce: in the bowl of a food processor fitted with a metal blade or in the container of a blender, process the drained apricots, lemon juice and salt until puréed. Reserve until ready to use.

3. To prepare the prune butter: in a large heavy-based saucepan over medium high heat, combine the chopped prunes, 125 ml (4 fl oz) water, the lemon juice and lemon zest and bring to the boil. Reduce the heat to low and simmer, covered, for 25 to 30 minutes, stirring often, until the prunes begin to fall apart and form a puree. Transfer the prune butter to a small heatproof bowl and reserve.

4. On a well-floured work surface, using well-floured finger-tips, roll the dough into twelve 4 cm (1½ in) balls. Using floured palms, flatten each ball into a 7.5 cm (3 in) wide round. Repeat until you have flattened all the balls, then place them between sheets of greaseproof paper on a baking sheet. Reserve until ready to use.

Dumplings:
325 g (11 oz) smoothly mashed
  potatoes (page 139)
2 size-3 egg yolks
1 teaspoon salt
Good pinch ground cloves
215 g (7½ oz) plain flour, plus
  more to dust

Apricot Sauce:
Makes 250 ml (8 fl oz) sauce
1 × 425 g (15 oz) can apricot
  halves, drained
1 tablespoon fresh lemon juice
Pinch salt

Prune Butter:
175 g (6 oz) stoned prunes, very
  finely chopped
1 tablespoon fresh lemon juice
1 teaspoon freshly grated lemon
  zest

(GERMANY)

Serves 4,

3 dumplings each

5. In a very large pan bring 5 litres (8 pints) of water to the boil. Pour 125 ml (4 fl oz) of the apricot sauce into a shallow baking dish. Preheat the oven to very low.

6. Place 2 teaspoonfuls of the prune butter in the centre of each dough round and draw the edges of the dough together over it while pushing in the filling, pinching firmly to seal and form a ball. Remove and discard any excess dough where pinched to create an even layer of dough all round. Repeat with the remaining dough and prune butter until you have 12 dumplings.

7. Drop a single layer of dumplings (about 4 to 6 per batch) at a time into the boiling water. Stir gently once or twice to prevent them from sticking to one another or the bottom of the pan. Boil for 7 to 9 minutes, or until they float to the surface. Using a slotted spoon, remove the batch of dumplings, drain in a colander and transfer to the baking dish. Pour some of the apricot sauce over the dumplings, tossing gently to coat them evenly. Transfer the dish to the oven to keep warm in between batches. Repeat the process with the remaining dumplings, adding each batch to the serving dish as they are done and drizzling with apricot sauce.

8. To serve divide the warm dumplings and sauce among 4 shallow soup bowls and serve at once.

Baked and Roasted

2

POTATO AND ROSEMARY TUILES

(FRANCE)

Makes about 20 biscuits

45 g (1½ oz) unsalted butter, at
room temperature, plus more
to grease baking sheets
1 tablespoon icing sugar
½ teaspoon salt
60 g (2 oz) smoothly mashed
potatoes (page 139)
1 size-3 egg white
60 g (2 oz) plain flour
2 teaspoons dried rosemary
2 tablespoons coarse sea salt, to
garnish

"That which was here-tofore reckon'd a food fit only for Irishmen and clowns is now become the diet of the most luxuriously polite."
—*Stephen Switzer,* Writing On Pota-toes, *1733*

1. Preheat the oven to 230°C (450°F or gas 8). Place a rack in the middle of the oven. Lightly butter a baking sheet.

2. In a medium bowl beat together the butter, sugar, the ½ teaspoon salt and mashed potatoes until well blended. Add the egg white, beating only briefly, just until blended.

3. Sift the flour into the bowl and gently fold it into the potato mixture until well blended.

4. Working quickly, drop teaspoonfuls of dough about 7.5 cm (3 in) apart on the buttered baking sheet. With the back of a spoon or rubber spatula, spread out each into a round about 7.5 cm (3 in) in diameter. (*Note:* The wafer should be even in thickness and not have any holes.) Sprinkle each round with a pinch of rosemary and a pinch of sea salt.

5. Bake for 5 to 7 minutes or until the edges are golden brown. Working quickly, using a palette knife, remove each wafer and place it rosemary side up on the rolling pin. Push it against the pin to mould the wafer into a curved shape. (*Note:* If the wafers crisp before you can mould them, return them to the oven for a few seconds to soften.) Transfer to a wire rack to finish cooling. Repeat with the remaining batter, re-greasing the baking sheet in between batches if needed. Serve at once, as an hors d'oeuvre or accompaniment to a lamb, beef, poultry or seafood dish.

POTATO PIROG

(Oval-Shaped Savory Pie)
(RUSSIA)

Serves 6

1. To prepare the dough: in a medium bowl cream together the butter and soft cheese until well blended and smooth. Beat in the soured cream just until well blended.

2. In a separate medium bowl sift together the flour, sugar and salt until combined. Stir the flour mixture into the cheese mixture until well blended and a soft dough forms. Transfer the dough to a lightly floured work surface and knead 3 or 4 times or just until smooth. Divide the dough into two equal parts and form each into a flat disc. Wrap separately in greaseproof paper and refrigerate for 1 hour, preferably overnight.

Dough:

120 g (4 oz) unsalted butter, at
  room temperature, plus more
  to grease
225 g (8 oz) soft cheese,
  preferably low-fat, at room
  temperature
4 tablespoons soured cream
300 g (10 oz) plain flour, plus
  more to dust
1 teaspoon caster sugar
½ teaspoon salt
1 size-3 egg, beaten with 1
  tablespoon milk, to glaze

Filling:

425 g (15 oz) mashed potatoes
  (page 139)
120 g (4 oz) soft cheese,
  preferably low-fat, at room
  temperature
4 spring onions, including
  7.5 cm (3 in) of green part,
  thinly sliced
60 g (2 oz) Parmesan cheese,
  freshly grated
½ teaspoon salt
¼ teaspoon freshly ground
  pepper
1 size-3 egg yolk, lightly beaten

3. To prepare the filling: in a medium bowl mix together the mashed potatoes and soft cheese until well blended. Stir in the spring onions, Parmesan cheese, salt, pepper and egg yolk until well blended.

4. Allow the dough to return to room temperature before rolling. On a lightly floured work surface, using a well-floured rolling pin, roll out one piece of the dough to an oval about 30 cm (12 in) long and 20 cm (8 in) wide and a uniform 3 mm (⅛ in) thickness. Transfer the dough to a lightly greased baking sheet. Repeat with the second dough disc, leaving it on the work surface until ready to use.

5. Spoon the potato filling in a 23 cm (9 in) long and 10 cm (4 in) wide mound down the centre of the dough on the baking sheet, leaving a 5 cm (2 in) margin on the sides and a 6 cm (2½ in) margin of dough at either end. Press gently down on the filling to mould it into a narrow, elongated shape. Using a pastry brush, paint some of the egg glaze along the edges of the filling. Lay the remaining sheet of dough over the filling and press the edges of the dough together to encase the filling. Trim the edges of the pastry, leaving a 2.5 cm (1 in) overhang, and crimp the edges to seal further. Use the dough trimmings to garnish the pie, cutting them into decorative shapes with a knife or pastry cutter. Brush the surface of the pie with the remaining egg glaze, sticking the shapes on in a pleasing pattern. Cut a 5 mm (¼ in) wide hole in the centre of the pie lid to allow steam to escape.

6. Preheat the oven to 220°C (425°F or gas 7).

7. Bake the pie for 30 to 40 minutes or until it is golden brown and sounds hollow when tapped. Serve at once.

450 g (1 lb) extra lean minced
  beef
1 medium onion, finely chopped
60 g (2 oz) smoothly mashed
  potatoes (page 139)
60 g (2 oz) cooked peeled beet-
  root or drained canned beet-
  root, finely chopped
2 teaspoons truffle mustard or
  Dijon mustard
1 tablespoon finely chopped
  fresh tarragon or 2 teaspoons
  dried, crumbled
½ teaspoon freshly ground
  pepper
4 bread rolls, split and heated or
  toasted, to serve
Hamburger accompaniments:
  lettuce, tomato, cheese of your
  choice, relish, tomato ketchup
  and mustard, to serve

> *"Potatoes, like wives,*
> *should never be taken*
> *for granted."*
>
> —*Peter Pirbright,*
> Off The Beaten
> Track, *1946*

1. Preheat the grill or prepare the barbecue.

2. To prepare the burgers: in a medium bowl gently stir together the beef, onion, mashed potatoes, beet-root, mustard, tarragon and pepper until well blended. Shape into 4 flat cakes, each 10 cm (4 in) in diameter. Reserve at room temperature until ready to use.

3. For the grill: grill under medium high heat for 4 to 5 minutes per side for rare, 5 to 6 minutes per side for medium-rare and 6 to 7 minutes per side for well done. (*Note:* cooking times are approximate. Cook until done to your taste and remember that the meat will still cook a little more even after it has been removed from the heat.)

4. For the barbecue: over hot coals, grill the hamburgers, about 12.5 cm (5 in) from the coals, for 3 to 4 minutes per side for rare, 4 to 5 minutes per side for medium-rare, and 5 to 6 minutes per side for well done.

5. To serve, assemble the hamburgers on rolls and serve with the various accompaniments, allowing the guests to help themselves.

SPUD BURGERS DELUXE

(AUSTRALIA)

Serves 4

★ POTATO BY ANY OTHER NAME ★

Here are some alliterative translations of international spud terminology:

Solanum tuberosum (Latin)	*Aardappel* (Dutch)	*Patata* (Italian)
Kentang (Indonesian)	*Cartof* (Romanian)	*Kartoffel* (Danish)
Patata, tartuffo (Spanish)	*Pomme de terre* (French)	*Bulvè* (Lithuanian)
Kartoffel, erdapfel (German)	*Kartofel* (Russian)	

 SWEET POTATO VINE BISCUITS

(UNITED STATES)

Makes about 30 small scones

300 g (10 oz) plain flour, plus
more to dust
2 teaspoons baking powder
½ teaspoon salt
60 g (2 oz) unsalted butter,
diced and chilled
250 g (9 oz) mashed yellow or
orange fleshed sweet potatoes
(page 133)
4 tablespoons milk
1 size-3 egg, beaten with 1
tablespoon milk, to glaze
3 tablespoons coarsely chopped
crystallised ginger, to garnish

1. In a medium mixing bowl sift together the flour, baking powder and salt. Using your fingertips rub in the chilled butter until the mixture resembles coarse crumbs. Stir in the mashed sweet potatoes and milk until the dough just clings together.

2. Preheat the oven to 230°C (450°F or gas 8).

3. On a lightly floured work surface, knead the dough gently for 10 to 12 turns or until it is well blended and smooth. Using a lightly floured rolling pin, roll out the dough to 5 mm (¼ in) thick. Using a floured 5 cm (2 in) biscuit cutter, cut the dough into rounds, dipping the cutter back into the flour between cuts when necessary. (*Note*: To insure straight-sided biscuits do not twist the cutter as you cut, or flatten the edges of the biscuits.) Re-roll scraps of dough and repeat the process until you have 30 biscuits.

4. Transfer the biscuits to an ungreased baking sheet, placing them 2.5 cm (1 in) apart. Brush the top of the biscuits lightly with the egg glaze and sprinkle the top of each with some of the crystallised ginger. Bake for 8 to 10 minutes or until the edges are very lightly browned. Serve at once.

2 medium aubergines, unpeeled
   and cut into 1 cm (½ in) thick
   slices (about 24 slices)
2 large boiling potatoes, washed
   thoroughly, peeled, and cut
   into 5 mm (¼ in) thick slices
   (about 12 slices)
Olive oil, to brush

Filling:
2 teaspoons olive oil, plus more
   to grease
1 medium onion, finely chopped
2 cloves garlic, crushed
225 g (8 oz) lean minced lamb
1 × 400 g (14 oz) can peeled
   whole tomatoes, crushed and
   drained
4 tablespoons brandy
½ teaspoon ground allspice
2 teaspoons finely chopped fresh
   oregano or 1 teaspoon dried,
   crumbled
Salt and freshly ground pepper
   to taste
1 × 225 g (8 oz) piece feta
   cheese, cut into 12 slices

1. Preheat the oven to 190°C (375°F or gas 5).

2. Lightly brush both sides of the aubergine and the potato slices with olive oil and transfer to 3 or 4 shallow baking pans (large enough to accommodate the aubergine and potato slices in a single layer). Bake for 25 to 30 minutes or until both the aubergines and potatoes are tender when pierced with a fork.

3. Meanwhile, prepare the filling: in a large heavy frying pan over medium heat, heat the olive oil. Add the onion and garlic and cook, stirring, for 3 to 4 minutes or until the onion is soft but not browned. Add the lamb and cook, breaking up the meat with the back of a wooden spoon, until the meat browns, about 7 to 10 minutes. Carefully pour off excess fat.

4. Return the pan to medium heat and stir in the tomatoes, brandy, allspice and oregano. Season with salt and pepper. Reduce the heat to low and simmer for 18 to 20 minutes, stirring occasionally, or until almost all the liquid has evaporated and the mixture has thickened.

INDIVIDUAL POTATO MOUSSAKAS

(GREECE)
Serves 6,
2 per serving

Topping:
Makes 350 ml (12 fl oz)
90 g (3 oz) unsalted butter
60 g (2 oz) plain flour
350 ml (12 fl oz) milk, at room
temperature

6 size-3 egg yolks, at room
temperature
120 g (4 oz) ricotta cheese
1 teaspoon freshly grated
nutmeg
Salt and freshly ground white
pepper to taste

5. Lightly grease 2 shallow baking pans. Arrange half the aubergine slices in a single layer in each pan. Spread 2 tablespoons of the filling to the edges on top of each aubergine slice. Then top each with a slice of potato followed by a slice of feta. Using the remaining aubergine slices, top each individual moussaka with an aubergine slice, matching the sizes of slices accordingly and pressing down to flatten slightly. (The recipe can be prepared up to this point 1 day ahead. Allow to cool, cover and refrigerate. Be sure to bring to room temperature before proceeding.)

6. To prepare the topping: in a large heavy-based saucepan over low heat, melt the butter. Whisk in the flour until large bubbles appear, about 3 minutes. Cook, whisking constantly, for 2 minutes more; do not let the *roux* brown. Gradually add the milk, still whisking constantly over the bottom and sides of the pan. Bring to the boil and boil for 4 minutes, whisking until smooth and thickened. In a small bowl whisk a little of the hot mixture into the egg yolks, then whisk this mixture back into the pan. Bring to the boil again, whisking constantly, and boil for 3 minutes, whisking until smooth and thick enough to pipe. Whisk in the ricotta cheese and nutmeg, season with salt and pepper and allow to cool to room temperature. Transfer to a piping bag fitted with a medium star tube and pipe a large rosette on top of each moussaka.

7. Bake for 30 to 35 minutes or until the topping is set. Serve hot.

49

BOURBON-GLAZED SWEET POTATO AND BANANA PONE

(UNITED STATES)

Serves 4 to 6

3 medium yellow or orange
   fleshed sweet potatoes (page
   133), cooked, peeled and cut
   in half lengthways
3 size-3 eggs
1 tablespoon molasses or treacle
½ teaspoon ground allspice
½ teaspoon freshly grated
   nutmeg
¼ teaspoon ground ginger
3 ripe but firm bananas, cut in
   half crossways, then halved
   lengthways
45 g (1½ oz) currants or
   seedless raisins
4 tablespoons bourbon whiskey
30 g (1 oz) unsalted butter,
   melted

1. Preheat the oven to 140°C (275°F or gas 1).

2. Arrange the cooked sweet potatoes in a single layer, cut side down, in a large round baking dish or gratin dish.

3. In a medium bowl whisk together the eggs, molasses, allspice, nutmeg and ginger until well blended. Pour this mixture over the potatoes in the baking dish.

4. Arrange the 12 banana slices over the potatoes in a pinwheel pattern, beginning at the centre of the dish. Sprinkle evenly with the currants and drizzle with the whiskey. Lightly brush the bananas evenly with the butter.

5. Bake for 40 to 50 minutes until the top is lightly browned. Serve hot from the baking dish, as a side dish to baked ham, roast pork or beef.

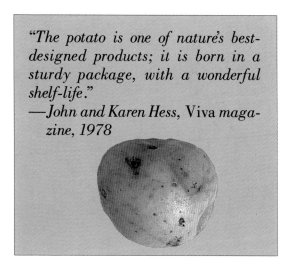

"The potato is one of nature's best-designed products; it is born in a sturdy package, with a wonderful shelf-life."
—*John and Karen Hess,* Viva *magazine, 1978*

1. To prepare the filling: in a large bowl combine the flour, salt and pepper and mix until well blended. Dredge the lamb in the seasoned flour until evenly coated, shaking off excess flour.

2. In a large heavy-based saucepan over medium high heat, heat the oil. Add the lamb in batches and sear, turning often so the cubes brown evenly on all sides, about 4 to 5 minutes per batch. Transfer the lamb to a medium bowl as it is browned and reserve.

3. Pour the stock into the saucepan (be careful—the liquid may splatter) and stir, scraping up the browned bits from the bottom and around the sides of the saucepan. Stir in the reserved lamb, red wine, tomato purée, mushrooms, carrots, sultanas, garlic, cumin, oregano and marjoram and season with salt and pepper. Bring to the boil. Reduce the heat to low and simmer for 15 minutes, stirring occasionally. Stir in the peas until well blended.

Filling:

30 g (1 oz) plain flour

¼ teaspoon salt

½ teaspoon freshly ground pepper

450 g (1 lb) lean boneless lamb, preferably from the shoulder, trimmed and cut into 2.5 cm (1 in) cubes

2 tablespoons sunflower or olive oil

250 ml (8 fl oz) beef stock, preferably home-made

175 ml (6 fl oz) dry red wine

2 tablespoons tomato purée

400 g (14 oz) button mushrooms, wiped clean with damp kitchen paper and thinly sliced

2 medium carrots or parsnips, cut into 3 mm (⅛ in) thick slices

75 g (2½ oz) sultanas or currants

3 cloves garlic, crushed

SHEPHERD'S PIE WITH ORANGE POTATO TOPPING

(BRITAIN)

Serves 4 to 6

1 teaspoon ground cumin

*1 tablespoon finely chopped
fresh oregano or 2 teaspoons
dried, crumbled*

*2 teaspoons finely chopped fresh
marjoram or 1 teaspoon dried,
crumbled*

*Salt and freshly ground pepper
to taste*

*½ cup fresh or thawed frozen
peas*

Topping:

*900 g (2 lb) smoothly mashed
potatoes (page 139), at room
temperature*

*150 ml (¼ pint) milk, plus more,
depending on consistency
needed to pipe*

*1 teaspoon freshly grated
orange zest*

¼ teaspoon salt

*¼ teaspoon freshly ground
white pepper*

2 tablespoons milk, to glaze

4. Preheat the oven to 190°C (375°F or gas 5).

5. Transfer the lamb mixture to a 23 cm (9 in) square baking dish that is 5 cm (2 in) deep, smoothing the top with a spatula.

6. To prepare the topping: in a large bowl mix together the mashed potatoes, milk, orange zest, salt and pepper until well blended. Transfer the topping to a piping bag fitted with a large star tube. Pipe 5 straight, parallel lines of topping 4 cm (1½ in) apart. Repeat, piping lines over the first group so that they form a lattice. Then pipe a large rosette of topping in every square to form a chec-querboard pattern.

7. Lightly brush the surface of the topping with the 2 tablespoons milk. Bake for 45 to 50 minutes or until the top is golden brown. Allow to stand for 10 minutes before serving. Serve hot from the baking dish.

7 g (¼ oz/scant 1 tablespoon)
   dried yeast
250 ml (8 fl oz) warm water
   (43°C/110°F)
2 tablespoons caster sugar
2 medium baking potatoes
   (page 132), cooked, peeled
   and coarsely mashed (enough
   to make 215 g/7½ oz)
5 tablespoons buttermilk
45 g (1½ oz) unsalted butter, at
   room temperature
2 teaspoons salt
2 cloves garlic, crushed
4 tablespoons finely chopped
   fresh dill
½ teaspoon cayenne pepper
700 g (1½ lb) strong plain flour,
   plus more to dust work surface
   and knead dough
Olive oil, to grease bowl and
   loaf tin

1. In a small heatproof bowl whisk together the yeast with the water. Add the sugar and whisk together until the yeast is dissolved. Set aside for 10 minutes or until the surface is frothy. (*Note*: If bubbles do not appear within 10 minutes, discard mixture and repeat process.)

2. Meanwhile, in a large bowl mix together the mashed potatoes, buttermilk, butter, salt, garlic, dill, cayenne pepper and 600 g (1¼ lb) of the flour until well blended. Stir in the yeast mixture and mix well until a soft, sticky dough forms.

3. Turn the dough on to a lightly floured surface; knead for about 10 minutes, adding the remaining flour, until elastic.

4. Lightly grease a large bowl with olive oil. Transfer the dough to the bowl and turn once to coat lightly with the oil. Cover with a towel and leave in a warm, draught-free place for 1½ hours or until doubled in size.

5. Lightly grease a 23 × 12.5 × 7.5 cm (9 × 5 × 3 in) loaf tin.

6. Transfer the dough to a lightly floured surface and gently knock it back. Knead it for 10 turns. Form it into a loaf and place in the loaf tin, seam side down. Cover with a towel and leave to rise for 30 to 40 minutes or until it has risen 2.5 cm (1 in) above the rim.

7. Preheat the oven to 180°C (350°F or gas 4).

8. Using kitchen scissors or a sharp knife, slash the top of the loaf with three 5 mm (¼ in) deep parallel incisions. Bake the loaf for 50 to 60 minutes or until golden brown on top and the bread sounds hollow when tapped.

9. Allow the bread to cool in the tin. Then remove from the tin and finish cooling on a wire rack before slicing.

ILLED BUTTERMILK POTATO BREAD   (UNITED STATES)

Makes a small loaf

Dough:

Olive oil, to grease bowl and
  pizza tin

2 medium baking potatoes
  (page 132), cooked, peeled
  and mashed (enough to make
  215 g/7½ oz)

225 g (8 oz) strong plain flour,
  plus more to dust work surface
  and knead dough

1 tablespoon finely chopped
  fresh sage or 1½ teaspoons
  ground dried sage

½ teaspoon salt

½ teaspoon freshly ground
  pepper

1 teaspoon dried yeast

125 ml (4 fl oz) warm milk
  (43°C/110°F)

½ teaspoon caster sugar

1. Lightly oil a 23 cm (9 in) pizza tin.

2. To prepare the dough: in a large bowl combine the mashed potatoes, flour, sage, salt and pepper. In a separate heatproof bowl whisk together the yeast with the milk. Add the sugar and whisk together until the yeast is dissolved. Set aside for about 10 minutes or until the surface is frothy. (*Note:* If bubbles do not appear within 10 minutes, discard mixture and repeat process.)

3. Stir the yeast mixture into the potato mixture and mix until a soft dough forms. Transfer the dough to a lightly floured work surface and knead for 8 to 10 minutes, or until dough is smooth and elastic. Lightly grease a medium bowl with the olive oil. Transfer the dough to the bowl and turn the dough once to coat it with the oil. Cover with a towel and leave in a warm, draught-free place for about 1½ hours or until doubled in size.

4. Transfer the dough to a lightly floured work surface. Then gently knock back the dough and knead 2 more turns. Place the dough on the oiled pizza tin and using your fingers press the dough out so it spreads uniformly to the edges to form

POTATO PIZZA WITH CARAMELISED SHALLOTS (ITALY)

Makes a 23 cm (9 in) pizza.
Serves 2, 3 slices per serving

an even crust. Pinch the edges to form a 2.5 cm (1 in) high rim completely encircling the pizza.

5. To prepare the topping: in a large heavy frying pan over medium heat, melt the butter. Add the shallots and cook, covered, stirring occasionally, for 20 minutes or until browned.

6. Stir in the sugar, vinegar, salt and pepper and cook, stirring, for 5 to 8 minutes or until the shallots are a deep golden brown. (The shallot mixture can be prepared up to 1 day in advance. Cool to room temperature, wrap and refrigerate.)

7. Preheat the oven to 220°C (425°F or gas 7).

8. Drain the shallot mixture and spread the mixture over the dough to the edges. Distribute the grated mozzarella over the top and sprinkle with the bacon. Bake for 15 to 20 minutes or until the cheese is melted and the dough is crisp and golden. Cut into 8 slices and place a whole basil leaf on each slice, the tip of the leaf pointing towards the centre. Serve at once.

> *"Many battles were fought. But sometimes after a battle the general looked at his muddied uniform and bent sword, and thought of a baked potato and a soft bed."*
> —*Anita Lobel*, Potatoes, Potatoes, *1967*

Topping:
60 g (2 oz) unsalted butter
350 g (12 oz) shallots, very thinly sliced
1 tablespoon caster sugar
2 tablespoons red wine vinegar
½ teaspoon salt
½ teaspoon freshly ground pepper
175 g (6 oz) mozzarella, grated
6 thin rashers streaky bacon, rinded, fried until crisp and crumbled, to garnish
8 whole fresh basil leaves, to garnish

HORIZO AND POTATO QUESADILLAS

(MEXICO)

Serves 4, 3 quesadillas
per serving

*2 teaspoons sunflower or
  vegetable oil*
*1 medium onion, coarsely
  chopped*
120 g (4 oz) fresh chorizo
  *(spicy pork-based sausage,
  sometimes smoked), very
  finely chopped*
*2 medium firm-fleshed potatoes
  (page 133), cooked, peeled
  and cut into 5 mm (¼ in)
  dice*
*2 large ripe tomatoes, peeled,
  seeded and finely chopped*
*1 to 2 fresh jalapeño peppers or
  other green chillies, seeded,
  ribs removed and very finely
  chopped*
½ teaspoon salt
*½ teaspoon freshly ground
  pepper*
*25 g (¾ oz) unsalted butter,
  softened at room temperature,
  plus more to grease*
*twelve 18 cm (7 in) flour
  tortillas (Source List,
  page 143)*
*120 g (4 oz) medium Cheddar
  cheese, grated*

*Soured cream or plain low-fat
  yogurt, to serve*
*Guacamole (Mexican avocado-
  based sauce), to serve*
*Salsa Picante (Mexican tomato
  sauce) or bottled taco sauce,
  to serve*

1. In a large heavy frying pan over medium high heat, heat the oil. Add the onion and *chorizo* and cook, stirring often, for 15 to 20 minutes or until the onion is golden and *chorizo* is browned evenly. Carefully pour off the fat.

2. Add the potatoes, tomatoes, chillies, salt and pepper and cook, stirring often, for 5 to 8 minutes or until the mixture is somewhat dry. Remove from the heat and reserve.

3. Preheat the oven to 200°C (400°F or gas 6). Lightly butter a baking sheet.

4. Lay the tortillas out on a work surface. Spread 4 table-spoons of the *chorizo* filling over half of each tortilla. Sprinkle the same half of each tortilla with the cheese. Fold the uncovered half of each tortilla over the filled half, gently pressing down on the filling to flatten and seal the tortilla closed, forming a half-moon.

5. Arrange the *quesadillas* on the buttered baking sheet about 2.5 cm (1 in) apart. Lightly brush the surface of each with the butter and bake for 10 to 15 minutes or until toasted and the edges are golden brown. Serve hot, with dollops of soured cream and guacamole on each. Serve the salsa or taco sauce separately.

Note: To prepare fresh chillies: the oil from chillies can act as an irritant, so wear rubber gloves and always wash your hands well after handling. Before cutting each chilli, rinse and remove the stalk under cold running water. Slice the chilli in half lengthways and discard the seeds. Using a sharp knife, remove and discard the white, fleshy ribs. The chilli is ready to be used according to recipe instructions.

SWEET POTATO SILVER DOLLARS

(UNITED STATES)

Serves 4, 8 small griddle cakes per serving

4 size-3 eggs

½ teaspoon salt

½ teaspoon baking powder

30 g (1 oz) plain flour

1 tablespoon caster sugar

250 g (9 oz) mashed yellow or orange fleshed sweet potato

45 g (1½ oz) unsalted butter, melted

4 tablespoons milk

¼ teaspoon ground cinnamon

Good pinch freshly grated nutmeg

1 teaspoon grated peeled fresh root ginger

2 tablespoons sunflower oil, to grease

Warm maple syrup or honey, to serve

Butter, to serve

1. In a medium bowl beat together the eggs, salt, baking powder, flour, sugar, mashed sweet potatoes, melted butter, milk, cinnamon, nutmeg and grated ginger until smooth.

2. Heat a medium non-stick frying pan or griddle over medium heat until very hot. (To test: flick water on to the hot pan. It is ready when the water drops bead and dance.) Coat frying pan lightly with the sunflower oil.

3. Drop tablespoonfuls of batter on to the pan, making sure that when they spread out they measure less than 7.5 cm (3 in) in diameter. Cook for 3 or 4 minutes or until a few bubbles appear on the surface of the cakes, then flip over and cook the other side for about 1 minute. Repeat with the remaining batter, adding more oil if needed to coat the pan in between batches. Keep the cakes in a very low oven to keep warm until ready to serve. Serve with warm maple syrup (or honey) and butter for guests to help themselves.

> *"There is no species of human food that can be consumed in a greater variety of modes than the potato."*
> —*Sir John Sinclair, 1828*

MALARABIA

*(Guava, Plantain, and
Sweet Potato Compote)*

350 ml (12 fl oz) guava nectar
   or juice blend (available at
   health food shop or
   supermarket)
4 tablespoons fresh lemon juice
3 medium yellow or orange
   fleshed sweet potatoes,
   cooked, peeled and cut into
   1 cm (½ in) dice
2 large ripe but firm plantains
2 tablespoons light soft brown
   sugar
2 tablespoons dark rum
½ teaspoon ground cinnamon
¼ teaspoon ground cloves
¼ teaspoon freshly grated
   nutmeg
¼ teaspoon ground allspice
125 ml (4 fl oz) canned cream
   of coconut

1. In a large non-reactive heavy-based saucepan over medium heat, combine the guava juice, lemon juice and sweet potatoes and bring to the boil.

2. Meanwhile, peel the plantains. Trim the ends of the fruit and cut the plantains in half lengthways. Remove and discard the fibre that runs down the centre of the fruit. Cut the plantains crossways into 5 mm (¼ in) thick slices.

3. Raise the heat to medium high. Stir the plantains, 125 ml (4 fl oz) water, the brown sugar, rum, cinnamon, cloves, nutmeg and allspice into the saucepan until well blended. Bring the mixture to the boil. Then reduce heat to low and simmer for 15 to 20 minutes more, stirring often, or until the plantains begin to fall apart and the mixture has thickened.

4. Remove the saucepan from the heat and transfer the mixture to a medium heatproof bowl. Stir a little of the hot mixture into the cream of coconut in a small bowl, then stir this mixture back into the remainder until well blended. Allow to cool to room temperature before serving. (The recipe can be made up to this point 3 days ahead. Cool, cover and refrigerate. Bring to room temperature before serving.) Serve with a pork, chicken or beef dish.

(PUERTO RICO)

Makes about 1.2 litres (2 pints)

Bread:
1 large baking potato, peeled
Sunflower oil or vegetable oil, to
grease tins
215 g (7½ oz) plain flour
1 tablespoon baking powder
135 g (4½ oz) caster sugar
45 g (1½ oz) unsweetened
cocoa powder
½ teaspoon salt
¼ teaspoon freshly ground
pepper
1 size-3 egg
120 g (4 oz) unsalted butter,
melted
Icing sugar, to garnish
(optional)

Orange Chocolate Butter:
Makes about 150 g (5 oz)
120 g (4 oz) unsalted butter, at
room temperature
1 tablespoon freshly grated
orange zest
30 g (1 oz) plain chocolate,
finely chopped

Raspberry jam, to serve
(optional)

1. To prepare the bread: place the potato directly on a rack or in a steamer basket in a large saucepan over 5 cm (2 in) of boiling water (the water level should not touch the bottom of the rack). Cover the saucepan and steam the potato for 25 to 30 minutes or until it is tender. Drain, reserving 350 ml (12 fl oz) water. Using a potato masher or potato ricer, mash the potato until smooth. You will need 215 g (7½ oz) mashed potato. Reserve the cooking liquid and mashed potato separately.

2. Preheat the oven to 180°C (350°F or gas 4). Lightly grease six 10 × 5 × 4 cm (4 × 2 × 1½ in) loaf tins or one 23 × 12.5 × 7.5 cm (9 × 5 × 3 in) loaf tin.

3. Sift together the flour, baking powder, sugar, cocoa powder, salt and pepper into a large bowl.

4. In a medium bowl beat together the egg, melted butter, the reserved mashed potato and potato cooking liquid just

★ SPUD SUPERSTITIONS OR LUMPER LORE ★

For a bountiful yield, potatoes should be planted in the dark of the moon.

Italian 'voodoo': write the name of your victim on a piece of paper and tack the paper to a potato. According to an old Italian superstition, the person will die a painful death within a month.

A potato flower (even though it is poisonous) means benevolence for its owner.

until combined. Pour the liquid mixture into the flour mixture and stir just until blended, being careful not to overmix.

5. Fill each miniature loaf tin two-thirds full, or fill the large loaf tin. Using a knife, smooth the top of each.

6. Bake the miniature loaves for 30 to 35 minutes, the large loaf for 45 to 50 minutes or until a wooden cocktail stick inserted into the centre comes out clean. Allow to stand for 10 minutes before serving. (The recipe can be made up to this point 2 days ahead. Allow to cool completely in tins. Remove from tins, wrap and refrigerate. Bring to room temperature before serving.)

7. Meanwhile, prepare the butter: in a small bowl beat the butter until soft. Stir in the orange zest and chocolate until well blended.

8. To serve, carefully remove the bread from the tins. Using a fine-mesh sieve, lightly dust the top of the bread with the icing sugar, if using. Serve warm or at room temperature, with the orange chocolate butter or raspberry jam if liked.

POTATO CHOCOLATE BREAD WITH ORANGE CHOCOLATE BUTTER

(UNITED STATES)

*Makes 6 miniature loaves
or 1 small loaf*

 WEET POTATO CUSTARD

Sunflower or vegetable oil, to
grease
90 g (3 oz) smoothly mashed
yellow or orange fleshed
sweet potatoes (page 136)
100 g (3½ oz) caster sugar
125 ml (4 fl oz) single or half
cream
125 ml (4 fl oz) skimmed milk
2 size-3 eggs
1 size-3 egg yolk
½ teaspoon ground cinnamon
¼ teaspoon ground cloves
¼ teaspoon ground ginger
¼ teaspoon freshly grated
nutmeg
¼ teaspoon salt
¼ teaspoon freshly ground pepper
45 g (1½ oz) sultanas or currants,
soaked in 2 tablespoons dark
rum for 15 minutes, drained and
excess rum discarded
1 litre (1¾ pints) boiling water
Rum-spiked fresh whipped
cream, to serve (optional)

> *"Never eat more than
> you can lift."*
>
> *—Miss Piggy*

(CARIBBEAN)
Serves 4

1. Preheat the oven to 180°C (350°F or gas 4). Liberally grease 4 heatproof ramekins (150 ml/¼ pint each) and arrange in a large baking tin.

2. In a medium bowl beat together the mashed sweet potatoes, sugar, cream, skimmed milk, eggs, egg yolk, cinnamon, cloves, ginger, nutmeg, salt and pepper until smooth. Stir in the drained sultanas until well blended. Divide the mixture evenly among the ramekins.

3. Carefully pour the boiling water into the corner of the baking tin, around the ramekins to a depth of 2.5 cm (1 in). Using oven gloves (the tin will be hot), transfer the tin to the middle rack of the oven and bake for 45 to 50 minutes or until a knife inserted near the centre comes out clean.

4. Remove the ramekins from the tin and allow to cool to room temperature. Cover and refrigerate the custards for at least 2 hours or until thoroughly chilled. (The recipe can be prepared up to this point 1 day ahead.)

5. To serve, run a knife around the inside of each ramekin to release the custard from the edge. Dip the bottom of the ramekin briefly in hot water, then wipe the outside dry. Invert on to a chilled dessert plate and serve with rum-spiked whipped cream.

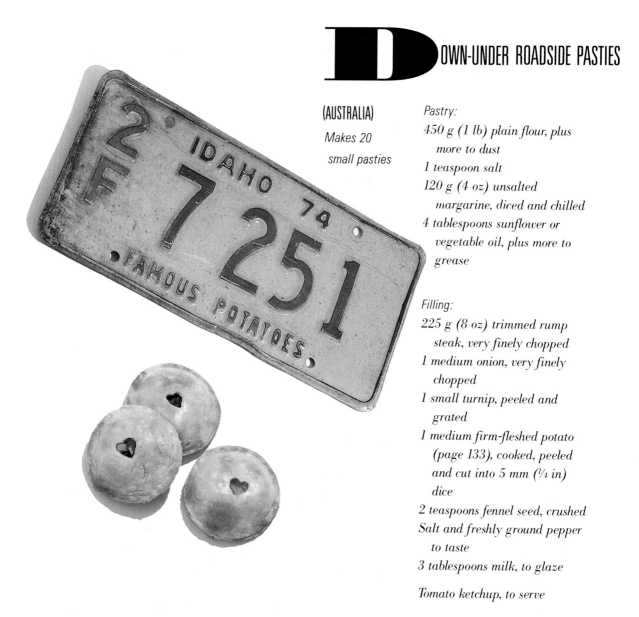

DOWN-UNDER ROADSIDE PASTIES

(AUSTRALIA)

*Makes 20
small pasties*

Pastry:

450 g (1 lb) plain flour, plus
   more to dust

1 teaspoon salt

120 g (4 oz) unsalted
   margarine, diced and chilled

4 tablespoons sunflower or
   vegetable oil, plus more to
   grease

Filling:

225 g (8 oz) trimmed rump
   steak, very finely chopped

1 medium onion, very finely
   chopped

1 small turnip, peeled and
   grated

1 medium firm-fleshed potato
   (page 133), cooked, peeled
   and cut into 5 mm (¼ in)
   dice

2 teaspoons fennel seed, crushed

Salt and freshly ground pepper
   to taste

3 tablespoons milk, to glaze

Tomato ketchup, to serve

1. To prepare the pastry: in a medium bowl sift together the flour and salt. Using your fingertips rub in the margarine until the mixture resembles coarse crumbs. Stir in the oil and 4 tablespoons water until a well blended and smooth, soft dough forms. Form into a flat disc and wrap in greaseproof paper. Refrigerate until ready to use.

2. Meanwhile, prepare the filling: in a medium bowl stir together the steak, onion and turnip until well blended. Stir in the potato and fennel seed and season with salt and pepper, stirring gently until well blended.

3. On a lightly floured work surface, using a well-floured rolling pin, roll out the dough to a uniform 3 mm (⅛ in) thickness. Using a floured biscuit cutter, cut the dough into 7.5 cm (3 in) rounds, dipping the cutter back into the flour in between cuts. Re-roll the scraps of dough and repeat until you have 40 rounds.

4. Preheat the oven to 200°C (400°F or gas 6). Lightly oil a baking sheet.

5. Place a dough round on the prepared baking sheet and place 1 heaping tablespoon of filling in the centre of the round. Using your fingers, lightly moisten the edge of the round with water, then place a second round on top. Using a fork, press the edges to crimp and seal them together. With a tiny round or shaped cutter punch out a hole in the top of the round to expose the filling or prick twice with a fork to allow steam to escape. Repeat with the remaining rounds and filling, placing the pasties 1 cm (½ in) apart on the baking sheet. Lightly brush each pasty with milk.

6. Bake for 30 to 35 minutes or until crisp and the edges are golden brown. Serve hot with tomato ketchup for guests to help themselves.

★ SPUD-TACULAR EXTRAVAGANZA ★

There is so much experimentation with new crops that it is next to impossible to get an accurate count of the types of potatoes now being grown. One source said that there are 400 varieties but less than 30 types are being cultivated. Another source said there are 10,000 types in existence, but I suppose all that matters is how many types reach your greengrocer! Some of the ancient potato varieties are being rediscovered. I call them 'heritage' potatoes. The names alone are better than lipstick colour names. Here is a sample: Pink Fir, French La Ratte, Siberian, Lady Fingers, Peanut, Tobique, Warba (Pink Eye), Viking Purple, Sangre, Huckleberry, Alaska Sweetheart, Caribe, Bison, Sunrise, Pink Pearl, Purple Peruvian, All Blue, Candy Stripe, Larota . . . I suspect that your shop could at any given time supply you with as many as 15 types (some will be early crops, others will be main crops). This is a good springboard for the culinary realisation of the potato's true potential. You won't be able to find all in your local greengrocer, but the potato is a bestseller, and its popularity is growing day by day. Smart shopkeepers are always expanding their range of varieties, so, if they don't have a particular type you want, just ask!

165 g (5½ oz) smoothly mashed
   potatoes (page 139)
5 size-3 eggs, separated
90 g (3 oz) shelled pecan nuts,
   very finely ground in a food
   processor fitted with a metal
   blade
90 g (3 oz) flavourful light-
   coloured honey
100 g (3½ oz) caster sugar
Sunflower oil or unsalted butter,
   to grease

Unsweetened whipped cream, to
   serve (optional)
Fresh ripe blackberries,
   raspberries, blueberries,
   strawberries or cherries, to
   serve (optional)

1. In a large bowl stir together the mashed potatoes, egg yolks, ground pecans and honey until well blended.

2. Preheat the oven to 170°C (325°F or gas 3). Lightly grease the bottom of 20 cm (8 in) cake tin and line with greaseproof paper or parchment paper. Lightly grease the top of the paper and side of the tin.

3. In another medium bowl combine the sugar and egg whites and whisk until they form stiff peaks. Working quickly, stir a little of the egg white mixture into the potato mixture, then fold the remaining egg whites into the potato mixture until well blended.

4. Pour the mixture into the prepared tin, smoothing the top. Place the tin on the middle rack of the oven and bake for 45 to 55 minutes or until a wooden cocktail stick inserted in the centre comes out clean.

5. Let the torte cool in the cake tin for 15 minutes. Then carefully run a knife round the edges to release the torte from the tin. Using two palette knives or your hands, very carefully lift the torte straight out on to a cake rack. (Do not invert torte to avoid marks from the rack on top of the torte.) Remove and discard the lining paper from the bottom of the torte. Allow to finish cooling to room temperature.

6. To serve, cut into wedges and serve at room temperature. Decorate each slice with a dollop of whipped cream and fresh berries or cherries if liked. To store: cool completely, wrap tightly and keep in an airtight tin at room temperature for up to 2 days.

(UNITED STATES)

Makes a 20 cm (8 in) torte,
serving 4 to 6

FLOURLESS HONEY PECAN POTATO TORTE

POTATO AND CHEESE STRUDEL WITH GLACE FRUIT

(GERMANY)

Serves 4 to 6

Filling:

60 g (2 oz) cottage cheese
4 tablespoons soured cream or
plain low-fat yogurt
100 g (3½ oz) smoothly mashed
potatoes (page 139)
2 tablespoons caster sugar
1 size-3 egg, lightly beaten
1½ teaspoons freshly grated
lemon zest
1 teaspoon vanilla essence
90 g (3 oz) assorted glacé or
dried fruits, finely chopped
Sunflower or vegetable oil, to
grease

Pastry:

Four 30 × 42.5 cm (12 × 17 in)
sheets of phyllo, stacked
between 2 sheets of
greaseproof paper and
covered with damp kitchen
paper
30 g (1 oz) unsalted butter,
melted
45 g (1½ oz) dried breadcrumbs
Icing sugar, to garnish
(optional)

1. To prepare the filling: in a medium bowl mix together the cottage cheese, soured cream, mashed potatoes, sugar and egg just until well blended; do not overmix. Stir in the lemon zest, vanilla essence and fruit until blended.

2. Preheat the oven to 180°C (350°F or gas 4). Line a baking sheet with parchment paper or lightly grease.

3. To prepare the pastry: place a tea towel with long side facing you on a work surface, cover it with one phyllo sheet and brush the sheet with a little of the butter. Working quickly, repeat the process with the remaining sheets of phyllo, layering them using a total of half of the melted butter. Sprinkle the phyllo evenly with the breadcrumbs, leaving a 5 cm (2 in) margin on all sides.

4. Spoon the cheese mixture on the breadcrumbs along the long side of the dough, leaving the 5 cm (2 in) margin uncovered. Working quickly, using the towel as a guide, roll up the strudel tightly lengthways, enclosing the filling. Carefully transfer the strudel seam side down to the prepared baking sheet. Trim the ends on the diagonal and discard them. Using a bread knife cut the strudel very lightly on the diagonal to score 8 equal portions, but do not cut all the way through the crust. Brush the entire surface of the strudel with the remaining melted butter.

5. Bake on the middle rack of the oven for 30 to 40 minutes or until crisp and lightly browned.

6. To serve, allow to stand for 10 minutes, then finish cutting through the strudel. Using a fine-mesh sieve lightly dust the top of each strudel portion with icing sugar if using. Or dust with sugar through a decorative pastry stencil. Serve hot or at room temperature.

Pastry:

Makes enough for 20 to 23 cm
* (8 to 9 in) tart shell*

215 g (7½ oz) plain flour, plus
* more to dust*

½ teaspoon salt

60 g (2 oz) butter or margarine

120 g (4 oz) smoothly mashed
* yellow or orange fleshed*
* sweet potato (page 135)*

3 to 4 tablespoons iced water

1. To prepare the pastry: into a medium bowl sift together the flour and salt. Using your fingertips rub in the butter and mashed sweet potato until the mixture resembles fine crumbs. Then stir in the iced water, a tablespoon at a time, as needed to allow dough to form but not become sticky. Form into a flat disc. Wrap in greaseproof paper and chill for at least 30 minutes until ready to use. (The dough can be prepared ahead, wrapped and refrigerated for up to 1 day. Bring to room temperature before proceeding with recipe.)

2. To prepare the filling: in a heatproof bowl set over a pan of barely simmering water, combine the chocolate and butter and melt. Remove from the hot water and allow to cool to room temperature.

3. Preheat the oven to 200°C (400°F or gas 6).

4. Meanwhile, on a lightly floured work surface, using a lightly floured rolling pin, roll out the dough 3 mm (⅛ in) thick. Trim to fit the bottom of a 20 to 23 cm (8 to 9 in) pie or tart tin with a 2.5 cm (1 in) overhang. Very lightly moisten the edges of the tin with water and line with the pastry (avoid stretching the pastry or it will shrink when baked). Fold under the extra pastry to build up the rim and crimp to form a pretty edge. Re-roll the scraps of dough and, using a cutter of your choice up to 8.5 cm (3½ in) in diameter, cut out

Chocolate Pecan Tart with Sweet Potato Crust

74

8 shapes to decorate the top of the pie. Transfer the decorations to a greaseproof paper-lined baking sheet and refrigerate until ready to use.

5. In a large bowl beat the eggs until light and fluffy. Beat in the sugar, golden syrup, maple syrup, vanilla essence and salt until well blended. Beat in the cooled chocolate mixture. Stir in the pecans until well blended.

6. Pour the filling into the tart shell. Decorate the surface of the filling with reserved pastry shapes, and sprinkle each with a little of the sugar if using. Transfer the tart to a baking sheet. Bake on the middle rack of the oven for 15 minutes. Reduce the heat to 180°C (350°F or gas 4) and bake for 30 to 40 minutes more, or until the centre of the filling is almost set. (*Note*: The very centre of the pie should be slightly soft, while the edges and near centre will be set.) Be careful not to overbake. The filling will set completely as the chocolate pecan tart cools.

7. To serve, allow the tart to stand for 15 minutes before cutting. Serve warm or at room temperature. Slice and serve with dollops of whipped cream decorated with chocolate curls if liked. To store: cool to room temperature, wrap tightly and refrigerate for up to 2 days. Return to room temperature before serving.

(UNITED STATES)

Makes a 20 to 23 cm (8 to 9 in) tart, serving 6 to 8

Filling:

90 g (3 oz) plain chocolate, finely chopped
60 g (2 oz) unsalted butter
3 size-3 eggs
150 g (5 oz) caster sugar
175 ml (6 fl oz) golden syrup or treacle
125 ml (4 fl oz) maple syrup
1½ teaspoons vanilla essence
¼ teaspoon salt
150 g (5 oz) pecan nut halves
Good pinch caster sugar, to garnish (optional)

Unsweetened whipped cream flavoured with good pinch ground ginger (optional)
Chocolate curls, to decorate (optional)

3

Mashed, Scalloped, and Au Gratin

CHINESE-STYLE MASHED POTATOES

(CHINA)

Serves 4

*450 g (1 lb) mashed potatoes
(page 139) from baked
potatoes*
3 tablespoons soy sauce
*2 tablespoons black sesame
seeds (available at Chinese
food shops) or white sesame
seeds, toasted in preheated
180°C (350°F or gas 4) oven
for 2 or 3 minutes, stirring
often*
1 tablespoon Oriental sesame oil
Freshly ground pepper to taste
*4 medium baked potato skin
shells (from scooped-out
baked baking potatoes)*
*Sunflower or vegetable oil, to
grease*
*90 g (3 oz) chow mein noodles
(deep-fried Chinese noodles,
available at Chinese food
shops)*

1. Preheat the oven to 180°C (350°F or gas 4).

2. In a medium bowl combine the mashed potatoes, soy sauce, sesame seeds and sesame oil. Season with pepper. Firmly pack one-quarter of the mashed potato mixture into each potato shell. Repeat until you have 4 filled potato shells. Transfer to a lightly greased baking sheet. Using one-quarter of the chow mein noodles, stud the top of each stuffed potato to resemble a porcupine. Bake for 10 to 15 minutes or until heated through.

3. Serve hot as an appetizer or as a side dish with a beef or pork main course.

> *"There are many ways to love a vegetable. The most sensible way is to love it well-treated. Then you can eat it with the comfortable knowledge that you will be a better man for it, in your spirit and your body too . . ."*
> —*M.F.K. Fisher,* How To Cook A Wolf, *1951*

SWISS-STYLE MASHED POTATOES

Sunflower or vegetable oil, to
grease
675 g (1½ lb) mashed potatoes
(page 139)
1 tablespoon redcurrant jelly
1 teaspoon freshly ground white
pepper
30 g (1 oz) unsalted butter,
melted
¼ teaspoon ground cinnamon
Good pinch ground cloves
1 × 425 g (15 oz) can pear
halves, drained and each pear
half cut in half lengthways,
syrup reserved

"What I say is, that
if a man really likes
potatoes, he must be
a pretty decent sort of
fellow."
—**A.A. Milne**, Not
That It Matters

(SWITZERLAND)
Serves 4

1. Preheat the oven to 180°C (350°F or gas 4). Lightly grease timbale moulds or ramekins (175 ml/6 fl oz each).

2. In a medium bowl combine the mashed potatoes, redcurrant jelly, pepper, melted butter, cinnamon and cloves until well blended. Divide the mixture among the moulds and pack it in firmly.

3. Invert each mould on to a lightly greased baking sheet and shake gently to help the mashed potato form loosen from the mould. Press 3 pear slices (uniform in size) cut side down into and around the sides of each mashed potato form in a vertical pattern, the tips of the pears meeting at the top. Repeat until you have 4 pear 'pyramids'.

4. Drizzle half of the reserved pear syrup, reserving the remaining half, over the pears and transfer the baking sheet to the oven. Bake for 15 to 20 minutes or until the pears and mashed potatoes are heated through.

5. To serve, drizzle the remaining pear syrup over the moulds and serve at once. These potato molds make a nice accompaniment to a chicken, seafood or pork dish.

350 g (12 oz) marinated artichoke hearts, drained and cut lengthways into eighths (available at delicatessens)

675 g (1½ lb) cooked wild rice

Salt and freshly ground pepper to taste

2 medium firm-fleshed potatoes, peeled and sliced crossways into 3 mm (⅛ in) thick slices, preferably using a food processor fitted with a slicing disc or a mandoline

250 ml (8 fl oz) home-made chicken stock

4 tablespoons dry vermouth or dry white wine

4 ripe but firm medium red or yellow tomatoes or a combination of both, very thinly sliced

30 g (1 oz) dried breadcrumbs

30 g (1 oz) Parmesan cheese, freshly grated

3 tablespoons olive oil, plus more to grease

(FRANCE)

Serves 4 to 6

POTATO, TOMATO, AND ARTICHOKE GRATIN ON BED OF WILD RICE

1. Preheat the oven to 220°C (425°F or gas 7). Lightly grease a 2 litre (3½ pint) gratin dish or baking dish.

2. In a medium bowl combine the artichoke hearts and cooked wild rice until well blended. Season lightly with salt and pepper. Transfer the artichoke mixture to the prepared gratin dish, smoothing evenly. Overlap the potato slices on top of the artichoke mixture in a pattern of parallel lines, but in a single layer. Season liberally with salt and pepper.

3. Pour the chicken stock and then the vermouth over the potatoes. Repeat the pattern of the potatoes with the tomatoes. If using both red and yellow, alternate the colours.

4. In a small bowl mix the breadcrumbs and cheese. Sprinkle over the gratin. Drizzle olive oil over all.

5. Bake for 10 minutes. Reduce the heat to 190°C (375°F or gas 5) and bake for 40 to 50 minutes more or until the top is golden brown and crusty. Serve hot from the dish.

1 tablespoon olive oil

1 medium onion, finely chopped

3 cloves garlic, finely chopped

3 medium carrots, grated

*575 g (1¼ lb) mashed potatoes
(page 139)*

*1½ tablespoons paprika,
preferably Hungarian sweet
paprika (Source Lists page
142)*

*8 thin rashers streaky bacon,
rinded, fried until crisp and
crumbled*

½ teaspoon salt

*½ teaspoon freshly ground
pepper*

*750 ml (1¼ pints) tomato sauce,
preferably home-made*

*2 medium green cabbages (a
total of 1.5 to 1.8 kg/3½ to
4 lb), tough outer leaves
removed and discarded,
remaining leaves separated,
blanched until tender and kept
immersed in cold water until
ready to use*

1. In a large heavy frying pan over medium high heat, heat the oil. Add the onion, garlic and shredded carrots. Cook, stirring often, for 5 to 7 minutes or until soft but not browned. Drain.

2. In a medium bowl combine the carrot mixture with the mashed potatoes, paprika, bacon, salt and pepper and mix until well blended.

3. Preheat the oven to 180°C (350°F or gas 4). Pour half of the tomato sauce into a 3 to 4 litre (5 to 7 pint) ovenproof casserole with a tight-fitting lid, preferably an unglazed clay cooker.

4. Drain the blanched cabbage leaves from the soaking water and choose the 12 largest leaves with the fewest tears, reserving the remaining leaves for another use. Place the leaves inner (hollow) side down next to each other on a work surface. Using a small sharp knife, slice off the raised part of the vein, as close as possible to the leaf. Then cut off the tip of the stalk and discard. Repeat with the remaining leaves, then flip each leaf over deveined side down.

5. Place a firmly packed 5 tablespoons of filling in the shape of a 6 cm (2½ in) long log 2.5 cm (1 in) above the stalk end of the leaf. Fold the stalk end of the leaf over the filling. Then fold the two sides of the leaf inwards and over the stuffing. Roll up the leaf tightly to enclose the filling. Place the cabbage bundle seam side down in the casserole with the tomato sauce. Repeat with the remaining 11 blanched cabbage leaves and filling, arranging them in a single layer.

6. Ladle the remaining tomato sauce over the cabbage bundles until coated. (The recipe can be prepared up to this point 2 days ahead. Cover and refrigerate. Bring to room temperature before proceeding with the recipe.) Bake, covered, for 30 to 40 minutes or until heated through. Serve hot.

★ SPUD SUPERSTITIONS ★ OR LUMPER LORE

The cure for a toothache: carry a potato in the pocket on the same side of the body as the sore tooth. The toothache will be cured when the potato has dried completely.

Lay slices of raw potato on irritated eyes to cure puffiness.

Rub a raw potato on your skin for sunburn relief or frostbite.

For protection against rheumatism and sciatica, wear a dried potato round your neck or carry it in your pocket.

To rid oneself of warts: rub the warts with a raw potato. Then bury or hide the potato. As the potato rots, the warts will fall off, one by one.

POTATO AND BACON-STUFFED CABBAGE BUNDLES

(POLAND)

Serves 4
3 bundles per serving

IRANIAN-STYLE CINNAMON SCALLOPED POTATOES WITH GRATED TURNIP

★ POTATO PARAPHERNALIA ★

Potato spikes (aluminum kitchen spikes inserted into a baking potato lengthways while it bakes, to promote an evenly baked potato)

Potato "eye" remover

Potato ricer

Potato masher

Potato fork (used to dig potatoes)

Potato peeler

Pommes Anna pan
(French copper pan made specifically for the dish *pommes Anna*, which was named for the French woman Anna Deslions and consists of overlapping potato slices resembling a flat cake)

---

30 g (1 oz) unsalted butter, melted

250 ml (8 fl oz) milk, at room temperature

1 teaspoon ground cinnamon

300 g (10 oz) shredded turnip (about 3 medium turnips)

Salt and freshly ground pepper to taste

4 medium baking potatoes, peeled and very thinly sliced lengthways, preferably sliced using a food processor fitted with a slicing blade or a mandoline

(IRAN)

Serves 4 to 6

1. Preheat the oven to 200°C (400°F or gas 6). Lightly grease a 2 litre (3½ pint) gratin dish or baking dish with a little of the melted butter.

2. In a medium bowl whisk together the milk and cinnamon until well blended.

3. Place the grated turnip in a small bowl and season liberally with salt and pepper, tossing until well blended. Spread the turnip mixture in the prepared gratin dish in a smooth even layer. Overlap the potato slices on top of the turnip mixture in a pattern of concentric circles and pour the milk mixture over all. Drizzle the remaining melted butter evenly over the top.

4. Bake for 20 minutes. Reduce the heat to 180°C (350°F or gas 4) and bake for 50 to 60 minutes more or until the potato and turnip mixture has absorbed most of the liquid and the top is golden brown and crisp. Serve hot from the dish to accompany pork, fish or chicken dishes.

ASHED POTATO AND THYME SOUP WITH POPCORN CROUTONS

(FRANCE)

Serves 4, about 175 ml
(6 fl oz) per serving

30 g (1 oz) unsalted butter
1 medium onion, very finely
    chopped
2 spring onions, white part only,
    thinly sliced
3 shallots, very finely chopped
600 ml (1 pint) chicken stock,
    preferably home-made
2 teaspoons finely chopped fresh
    thyme or fresh tarragon
450 g (1 lb) smoothly mashed
    potatoes (page 139)
4 tablespoons dry white wine
Salt and freshly ground white
    pepper to taste
Popped popcorn, to garnish
3 tablespoons finely chopped
    fresh chives, to garnish

1. In a large heavy-based saucepan over medium high heat, melt the butter. Add the onion, spring onions and shallots and cook, stirring, for about 3 or 4 minutes or until soft but not browned. Stir in the stock and thyme and bring to the boil, stirring occasionally.

2. Gradually stir in the potatoes. Bring to the boil again. Reduce the heat to low, stir in the wine and simmer for 5 minutes, stirring once or twice. Season with salt and pepper. Divide the soup among 4 shallow soup bowls and garnish each with popcorn and chives. Serve at once.

> *"Potato: bland, amiable, and homely, an honest vegetable, giving honour where honour is due—in an honest soup."*
> —Della Lutes, The Country Kitchen, 1938

Dough:

*450 g (1 lb) smoothly mashed
    potatoes (page 139)*

2 size-3 eggs, lightly beaten

*30 g (1 oz) unsalted butter,
    melted, plus more to grease*

*3 tablespoons very finely
    chopped onion*

*215 g (7½ oz) plain flour, plus
    more to dust*

½ teaspoon salt

*¼ teaspoon freshly ground
    white pepper*

Filling:

*2 tablespoons sunflower or
    vegetable oil*

1 medium onion, finely chopped

*225 g (8 oz) mushrooms, finely
    chopped*

*1 teaspoon finely chopped fresh
    thyme or ½ teaspoon dried*

½ teaspoon salt

*½ teaspoon freshly ground
    pepper*

*250 ml (8 fl oz) cooked medium
    kasha (roasted buckwheat
    groats) (see below)*

*4 tablespoons finely chopped
    fresh parsley*

1 size-3 egg yolk, lightly beaten

*Soured cream or plain low-fat
    yogurt, to serve (optional)*

POTATO AND KASHA KNISHES

(RUSSIA)

Makes 24 knishes

1. To prepare the dough: in a medium bowl combine the mashed potatoes, eggs, melted butter and onion. Stir in the flour, salt and pepper and mix gently until well blended and a smooth dough forms.

2. On a well-floured work surface, using a well-floured rolling pin, roll out the dough to a uniform 5 mm (¼ in) thickness. Cut the dough into 7.5 cm (3 in) rounds, using a floured pastry cutter, dipping the cutter back into the flour between cuts. Re-roll the scraps of dough and repeat the process until you have 24 rounds. Reserve at room temperature until ready to use.

4. Meanwhile, prepare the filling: in a large heavy frying pan over medium high heat, heat the oil. Add the onion, mushrooms, thyme, salt and pepper. Cook, stirring often, for 5 to 8 minutes or until the mushrooms release their liquid and begin to brown. Remove the pan from the heat and stir in the cooked kasha and parsley until well blended.

5. Preheat the oven to 180°C (350°F or gas 4). Lightly butter a baking sheet.

6. Place a dough round on the buttered baking sheet. Place 2 heaping teaspoons of filling in the centre of the round and draw the edges together over it, while pushing in the filling. Pinch firmly to seal to form a ball. Flip the knish over seam side down. Repeat the process with the remaining rounds and filling, placing the knishes 1 cm (½ in) apart on the baking sheet. Lightly brush the surface of each knish with the beaten egg yolk and bake for 40 to 45 minutes or until crisp and the top is golden brown. Serve at once, with soured cream if liked.

To Prepare Kasha

Makes 250 ml (8 fl oz)
1 size-3 egg, lightly beaten
60 g (2 oz) medium kasha
  (roasted buckwheat groats)
125 ml (4 fl oz) boiling water

In a small bowl combine the egg and kasha and stir until the grains are well coated. Place the kasha in a heavy-based medium frying pan over high heat. Using a wooden spoon, stir the kasha vigorously for 3 to 4 minutes or until the egg has dried and the grains separate. Remove the pan from the heat and add the boiling water all at once (be careful—the liquid may splatter), stirring until well blended. Reserve at room temperature until ready to use.

★ A POTATO HANGOVER? ★

Here are a few facts on intriguing potato-based alcoholic beverages:

Aquavit is a flavoured Scandinavian liquor. The traditional beverage of choice for the *skal* (toast) at a smorgasbord is *aquavit*, 'the water of life.' It is distilled from fermented potato or grain mash and usually contains a 42 to 45 percent alcohol content by volume. Some of the many flavourings include: caraway or cumin seed, lemon or orange peel, cardamom, aniseed and fennel.

Poteen is the Irish word for a potato-based liquor with a very high alcohol content, usually distilled illegally.

Chicha, which is a Peruvian beer, is made with potatoes.

F.Y.I.

★ Both Russian vodka and schnapps have been made with potatoes.

★ It has been said that wines made with a potato base have the potential, with some careful aging, to be as smooth as fine brandy.

SHAKER-STYLE STEWED POTATOES

(UNITED STATES)
Serves 2 to 4

3 medium firm-fleshed potatoes
    (page 132), cooked, peeled
    and cut into 1 cm (½ in) thick
    slices
250 ml (8 fl oz) milk
30 g (1 oz) unsalted butter, at
    room temperature
Salt and freshly ground pepper
    to taste

In a large heavy-based saucepan over medium low heat, combine the potatoes and milk and bring to the boil. Boil gently for 20 to 25 minutes, stirring occasionally, or until the mixture has thickened and the potatoes have absorbed all the milk. (*Note*: Stir gently so as not to break the potatoes.) Stir in the butter until well blended and season with salt and pepper. Serve at once, as an accompaniment to a poultry, fish or beef dish.

POTATO GAMES

★ "SPUD" Any number of people can play this dodge ball game, which keeps score by "spuds," or points against a person.

★ "COUNTING RHYME," which decides who is to be team captain before the start of a game. One player stands in the middle of a circle made by the other players. Each player clenches his fists, holding them out in front of him. The player in the center begins the selection by gently tapping his own fists together, then to the other players' fists in the circle (to the beat of the following rhyme). When a person's fists are tapped while the word "more" is said he is out of the circle. (Even if the counter is out, he can still continue counting.) The count continues until there is only one person left in the circle. That person becomes the team captain.

Rhyming Jingle: *ONE* potato, *TWO* potato, *THREE* potato, *FOUR. FIVE* potato, *SIX* potato, *SEVEN* potato, *MORE!*

SKORDALIA

(Garlic Sauce or Dip)

(GREECE)

Makes about 800 ml (1⅓ pints)

2 medium heads garlic, peeled
450 g (1 lb) smoothly mashed
  potatoes (page 139)
250 ml (8 fl oz) olive oil
150 ml (¼ pint) white wine
  vinegar
½ teaspoon salt
150 g (5 oz) Greek Kalamata
  olives or other brine-cured
  olives, rinsed, stoned and
  halved lengthways, to garnish
  (optional)

In the bowl of a food processor fitted with a metal blade, or in a blender, process the garlic until very finely chopped. Add the potatoes, half of the olive oil, the vinegar and salt and process just until blended. With the machine running, through the feed tube gradually pour in the remaining olive oil in a slow, steady stream and process until incorporated and the sauce is completely smooth. (*Note*: This sauce should have a mayonnaise-like consistency.)

(The recipe can be made up to this point 1 day ahead. Cover and refrigerate. Whisk and adjust seasoning to taste before serving.) Serve at room temperature or chilled, and garnish with the olives if desired. *Skordalia* can be used as a sauce for seafood, meat or vegetables or it can be served as a dip accompanied by crudités and hot pita bread.

★ OTHER INTERNATIONAL MASHED POTATO DISHES ★

★ Chilean-Style: Combine cooked pumpkin, fried rice and mashed potatoes.

★ French-Style: Combine slices of *foie gras* and mashed potatoes.

★ Brazilian-Style: Combine cooked peeled prawns and mashed potatoes.

★ Indian-Style: Combine chopped fresh mint and mashed potatoes.

*30 g (1 oz) butter, plus more to
grease*
*3 medium onions, very thinly
sliced*
*2 medium baking potatoes,
peeled and cut crossways into
3 mm (⅛ in) thick slices,
preferably using a food
processor fitted with a slicing
disc or a mandoline. (Note:
The slices should be thin
enough to see the outline of
the knife through them.)*
3 size-3 eggs
*350 ml (12 fl oz) milk, at room
temperature*
1 tablespoon dry sherry
1 teaspoon dry mustard
¼ teaspoon salt
*½ teaspoon freshly ground
white pepper*
½ teaspoon celery seed

1. In a large heavy frying pan over medium high heat, melt the butter. Add the onions and cook, stirring often, for 10 to 12 minutes or until they begin to brown. Cover and cook, stirring once, for 5 to 7 minutes more or until the onion is golden brown. Stir in the potatoes and cook, uncovered, gently stirring often, for 6 to 8 minutes more until the potatoes are tender. Reserve.

2. Preheat the oven to 190°C (375°F or gas 5). Butter a 2 litre (3½ pint) baking dish.

3. In a medium bowl whisk together the eggs, milk, sherry, dry mustard, salt, pepper and celery seed until well blended. Stir in half of the Gruyère cheese.

4. Transfer the onion and potato mixture to the baking dish and spread evenly. Pour the egg mixture over it and sprinkle the remaining Gruyère cheese evenly over the top.

5. Bake for 35 to 45 minutes or until set and the top is golden brown. Cut the pudding into squares, sprinkle with the parsley and serve hot with a beef or chicken dish.

FARMERS' POTATO AND ONION PUDDING

(UNITED STATES)
Serves 4 to 6

*120 g (4 oz) Gruyère,
Emmenthaler or Appenzeller
cheese, grated*
*1 tablespoon finely chopped
fresh parsley, to garnish*

1 tablespoon sunflower or
vegetable oil, plus more to
grease

1 medium onion, finely chopped

225 g (8 oz) extra lean minced
beef

225 g (8 oz) lean minced pork

1 tablespoon tomato purée

½ teaspoon cayenne pepper

½ teaspoon salt

½ teaspoon freshly ground
pepper

90 g (3 oz) black olives,
preferably Greek Kalamata
olives or other brine-cured
olives, stoned and finely
chopped

2.6 kg (5¾ lb) smoothly mashed
potatoes (page 139),
preferably from purple-fleshed
Peruvian potatoes (page 132)

6 hard-boiled eggs, cut in half
crossways

150 g (5 oz) unsalted peanuts,
finely chopped

1. In a large heavy frying pan over medium high heat, heat the oil. Add the onion and cook, stirring often, for 3 to 4 minutes or until soft but not browned. Add the minced beef, minced pork and tomato purée. Cook, stirring often to break up the lumps, for 10 to 12 minutes or until the beef and pork begin to brown. Carefully pour off the fat from the pan. Stir in the cayenne, salt and pepper. Stir in the olives and cook for 5 minutes more, stirring occasionally.

2. Using about 215 g (7½ oz) mashed potatoes per ball, form the mashed potatoes into 12 balls. Using a large spoon, hollow out each ball, so that the walls are 5 mm (¼ in) thick. Stuff each hollow with 3 tablespoons of the meat mixture, firmly packing it down into the ball. Then insert a hard-boiled egg half into the hole. Seal the hole with the potato mixture, re-forming the ball. Turn the ball over seam side down and smooth the surface while shaping the ball. Repeat with the remaining potato and meat mixture until you have 12 stuffed potato balls.

3. Preheat the oven to 190°C (375°F or gas 5).

4. Divide the peanuts among the 12 balls, pressing them in the shape of a small circle into the surface of each ball. Repeat with the remaining balls and transfer the balls to a lightly greased baking sheet, placing them 5 cm (2 in) apart. Bake for 25 to 30 minutes or until the peanuts are a light brown. Serve hot as a main dish.

PERUVIAN-STYLE STUFFED POTATO BALLS

(PERU)

*Serves 6, 2 balls
per serving*

90 g (3 oz) unsalted butter, plus
  ½ teaspoon to grease moulds
2 tablespoons freshly grated
  Parmesan cheese
175 g (6 oz) small fresh wild
  mushrooms
215 g (7½ oz) smoothly mashed
  potatoes (page 139)
120 g (4 oz) Gruyère cheese,
  grated
3½ tablespoons finely chopped
  fresh chives, plus 1 teaspoon
  to garnish
2 teaspoons Dijon mustard
1 teaspoon salt
½ teaspoon freshly ground
  white pepper
5 tablespoons plain flour
250 ml (8 fl oz) milk, heated
6 size-3 eggs, separated, at room
  temperature
1 teaspoon fresh lemon juice

1. Preheat the oven to 200°C (400°F or gas 6). Liberally butter the inside and rims of 4 individual soufflé moulds or ramekins, each 350 ml (12 fl oz), with the ½ teaspoon butter and arrange on a baking sheet. Sprinkle each with ½ tablespoon Parmesan cheese to coat the bottom and sides evenly. Refrigerate until ready to use.

2. In a small heavy frying pan over medium high heat, melt 30 g (1 oz) of the butter. Raise the heat to high, add the mushrooms and sauté just until golden brown, about 3 minutes. Using a slotted spoon, remove 12 of the prettiest mushrooms for garnish and reserve. Transfer the remaining mushrooms along with the mashed potatoes, Gruyère cheese, the 3½ tablespoons chives, mustard, salt and pepper to a large bowl and stir gently until well blended.

3. In the frying pan over medium heat melt the remaining 60 g (2 oz) butter. Whisk in the flour and cook, whisking constantly across the bottom and round the sides, for 2 minutes. Do not allow the *roux* to brown. Gradually whisk in the hot milk. Bring to the boil, whisking constantly, and cook for about 2 minutes, or until the mixture is as thick as paste. Remove from the heat and whisk in the egg yolks, one at a time, until well blended. Then gently stir the sauce mixture into the potato mixture, until well blended.

4. In a medium bowl whisk the egg whites with the lemon juice until stiff but glossy, not dry or grainy. Stir about one-quarter of the whites into the soufflé base until well blended. Working quickly and lightly, fold the remaining egg whites into the lightened whisked base. Spoon the mixture into the prepared chilled soufflé dishes. Immediately return the dishes to the baking sheet and transfer to the rack in the lower third of the oven. Bake the soufflés for 30 to 35 minutes or until puffy and the tops are crisp and golden brown. Divide the 12 reserved mushrooms and 1 teaspoon chives among the soufflés for garnish. Serve at once.

INDIVIDUAL POTATO AND CHEESE SOUFFLÉS WITH WILD MUSHROOMS

(FRANCE)

*Makes 4
individual soufflés*

Cake:

225 g (8 oz) plain flour

300 g (10 oz) caster sugar

1 teaspoon baking powder

1 teaspoon bicarbonate of soda

1 teaspoon salt

1½ teaspoons ground cinnamon

½ teaspoon ground mace

½ teaspoon ground cloves

¼ teaspoon ground ginger

¼ teaspoon freshly ground pepper

6 medium carrots, cooked until
*   very tender and puréed*

175 ml (6 fl oz) corn oil, plus
*   more to grease*

4 size-3 eggs, lightly beaten

Icing:

Makes about 350 ml (12 fl oz)

225 g (8 oz) soft cheese,
*   preferably low-fat, at room*
*   temperature*

30 g (1 oz) unsalted butter, at
*   room temperature*

225 g (8 oz) mashed potatoes
*   (page 139); combine with 2*
*   teaspoons water and purée in*
*   a blender container or food*
*   processor fitted with a metal*
*   blade until very smooth*

150 g (5 oz) icing sugar

½ teaspoon vanilla essence

3 tablespoons fresh orange juice

1 medium carrot, grated

CARROT AND POTATO TEA CAKES

(UNITED STATES)

Makes 12 to 16 tea cakes

1. Preheat the oven to 180°C (350°F or gas 4). Lightly grease the bottom of a 33 × 23 × 5 cm (13 × 9 × 2 in) baking tin. Line with greaseproof paper or parchment paper and lightly grease the top of the paper and sides of the tin.

2. To prepare the cake: in a large bowl sift together the flour, caster sugar, baking powder, bicarbonate of soda, salt, cinnamon, mace, cloves, ginger and pepper. Add the puréed carrots, oil and eggs and beat just until well blended, being careful not to overmix.

3. Pour the mixture into the prepared tin, smoothing the top. Lightly tap the base of the tin on the work surface to remove large air bubbles. Bake on the middle rack of the oven for 35 to 40 minutes, or until a wooden cocktail stick inserted in the centre comes out clean.

4. Allow the cake to cool in the baking tin for 15 minutes. Then carefully invert it on to a cake rack. Remove and discard the lining paper. Leave it to cool completely, approximately 1 hour.

5. Meanwhile, prepare the icing: in a medium bowl cream together the soft cheese, butter and puréed potatoes. Gradually sift in the icing sugar, beating well after each addition, scraping down the sides of the bowl as needed, until the icing is well blended and smooth. Beat in the vanilla essence and orange juice until well blended and fold in the grated carrots. Refrigerate until ready to use. (The icing can be made up to 1 day ahead. Cover and refrigerate.)

6. Transfer the cake to a sheet of greaseproof paper, carefully sliding it off the rack on to the paper. Using an 8.5 cm (3½ in) diameter pastry cutter in a simple shape (easier to cut cake) of your choice, carefully cut out 12 to 16 pieces of cake as close as possible to one another so as not to waste cake. (*Note*: The number of portions depends on the shape of the cutter.)

7. To serve, brush off any loose crumbs from the surface of the cakes and ice the top and sides of each one. Serve at room temperature or chilled. To store: arrange in a single layer in a large deep tin, cover so as not to disturb the icing and refrigerate for up to 2 days.

"Did you know that they (the Inca) measured their units of time by the time it takes a potato to cook?"
—Jane Grigson, Jane Grigson's Vegetable Book, *1979*

Sautéed and Fried

4

UBBLE AND SQUEAK

2 tablespoons olive oil

225 g (8 oz) onions, finely
  chopped

175 g (6 oz) Savoy or green
  cabbage (about ¼ small
  cabbage), finely shredded

1½ tablespoons strong coarse
  mustard

450 g (1 lb) smoothly mashed
  potatoes (page 139)

1 teaspoon salt

½ teaspoon freshly ground
  pepper

4 × 5 mm (¼ in) thick slices
  boiled or roast beef or roast
  pork, at room temperature
  (optional)

*"Whenever I fall in love,
I begin with potatoes."*

—Nora Ephron,
Heartburn

(ENGLAND)

Serves 4

1. In a large heavy frying pan over medium high heat, heat 1 tablespoon of the olive oil. Add the onion and shredded cabbage and cook, stirring, for 8 to 10 minutes or until lightly browned. Stir in the mustard, mashed potatoes, salt and pepper until well blended. Using a fish slice, spread the mixture into an even, firmly packed flat 'cake'. With the slice, push the edges of the cake up to form a raised edge. Cook about 5 to 7 minutes or until the bottom is golden brown. (*Note:* You will hear the 'bubbling' and 'squeaking' noise of the ingredients sizzling in the pan.)

2. Carefully place a heatproof plate on top of the pan and invert the cake on to the plate. Add the remaining tablespoon of olive oil to coat the frying pan. Slide the cake, browned side up, back into the pan. Cook the second side for 4 to 5 minutes or until golden brown. (*Note:* The centre should remain moist.) Using the fish slice, transfer the whole cake to a platter. Or cut it into 4 wedges, and place each wedge on a slice of beef or pork if using. Serve at once.

POTATO POTPOURRI

Since 1948, the motto of the Idaho state license plate has been Famous Potatoes.

In the 1840's, "potato trap" was slang for the word "mouth."

A potatophile is a person who loves potatoes.

The potato was valued in Europe as an aphrodisiac.

2 tablespoons usli ghee *(Indian clarified butter — see below) or olive oil*

1 medium onion, finely chopped

3 cloves garlic, finely chopped

1½ tablespoons grated peeled fresh root ginger

1¼ teaspoons ground cinnamon

1¼ teaspoons ground coriander

1 teaspoon ground turmeric

¾ teaspoon ground cumin

½ teaspoon dried hot red pepper flakes

¼ teaspoon ground cloves

¼ teaspoon freshly grated nutmeg

4 ripe medium tomatoes, peeled, seeded and coarsely chopped

4 medium firm-fleshed potatoes, peeled and cut into 1 cm (½ in) dice

4 tablespoons canned unsweetened coconut milk, not canned cream of coconut

120 g (4 oz) frozen peas, thawed

Salt and freshly ground pepper to taste

Fresh coriander leaves, to garnish

Cooked rice, preferably basmati rice, to serve

Selection of Indian condiments — dal, cucumber raita, Indian pickles and chutneys — to serve

1. In a large heavy frying pan over medium high heat, heat the *usli ghee*. Add the onion and garlic and cook, stirring, for about 4 minutes or until soft but not browned.

2. Reduce the heat to very low, and stir in the ginger, cinnamon, ground coriander, turmeric, cumin, pepper flakes, cloves and nutmeg. Cook, stirring, for 2 minutes. Add the tomatoes and cook, stirring often, for 5 minutes.

3. Raise the heat to medium and stir in the potatoes and 175 ml (6 fl oz) of water. Cook, covered, stirring often, for 20 to 25 minutes or until the potatoes are tender but not mushy. (The recipe can be made up to this point 1 day ahead. Cool, cover and refrigerate. Reheat over very low heat before proceeding with recipe.)

4. Stir in the coconut milk and peas and cook, uncovered, stirring often, for 3 minutes or until the peas are heated through. Season with salt and pepper. Serve hot, garnished with the fresh coriander. Accompany with cooked rice and a selection of Indian condiments.

To make *usli ghee*: in a large heavy-based saucepan over low heat, gently melt 225 g (8 oz) of diced unsalted butter, stirring occasionally. When a thin layer of white foam forms on the surface (about 10 minutes), simmer for 5 minutes or until the foam subsides. Then simmer for 25 to 35 minutes more, stirring often, until the mixture turns golden brown. Immediately remove the saucepan from the heat, transfer the butter to a heatproof bowl and allow to stand until the brown solids settle to the bottom.

When the butter is cool enough to handle, strain it through a sieve lined with a double layer of muslin into a heatproof bowl. Allow to cool completely, transfer to an airtight container and seal. Refrigerate for up to 2 months or freeze up to 6 months. Makes about 175 ml (6 fl oz).

OTATO CURRY

4 medium firm-fleshed potatoes,
    peeled
1 medium onion
2 size-3 eggs, lightly beaten
1 teaspoon salt
½ teaspoon freshly ground
    white pepper
¼ teaspoon celery seed
45 g (1½ oz) unsalted matzo
    meal or 75 g (2½ oz) plain
    flour
500 ml (16 fl oz) sunflower or
    vegetable oil
Apple sauce, preferably home-
    made, to serve

Latkes

(Jewish Potato Cakes)

(UNITED STATES)
*Serves 4, 3 or 4 cakes
per serving*

POTATO POTPOURRI

In the 1930's a potato was American slang for a dollar.

In Scotland in the year 1728 the potato was forbidden by law since it was not mentioned in the Bible and, therefore, deemed an unholy plant.

It takes 5 tonnes of raw potatoes to make 1 tonne of crisps.

The word spud was derived from the English gardening tool called spud, which is used for digging up roots.

Historically, Jewish families less wealthy than others were known to use a potato as a *menorah*—the candelabrum used in the Jewish celebration of Chanukah.

1. Shred the potatoes into long thin strips using the shredding disc of a food processor or the large holes on a 4-sided box grater. As you shred the potatoes, completely immerse the shreds in a bowl of cold water to prevent discoloration. Grate the onion and reserve in a medium bowl.

2. Add the eggs, salt, pepper, celery seed and matzo meal to the grated onion. Drain the potatoes and using your hands squeeze out any excess water. Combine the potatoes with the egg mixture, gently stirring them together until well blended, but do not overmix.

3. In a large heavy 25 cm (10 in) frying pan over medium high heat, heat the oil. (*Note*: You should have enough oil to make a 1 cm (½ in) deep layer.) Working quickly, with your hands form 2 heaping tablespoonfuls of the potato mixture into a flat 7.5 cm (3 in) wide cake, squeezing out excess liquid while you do so. Repeat with the remaining batter until you have 12 to 16 potato cakes. (*Note*: To test the readiness of the oil drop a teaspoon of the batter into the oil; it should take about 30 seconds to brown each side.) Fry the potato cakes in batches of 2 or 3 (do not crowd the pan) about 3 to 4 minutes per side or until crisp and golden brown. Drain each batch on kitchen paper. Serve at once with apple sauce.

POTATO POTPOURRI

F.D.A. (United States Food and Drug Administration) surveys show that as of 1990 the average American eats 53.7 kg (124 lb) of potatoes per year while the average European consumes twice that much!

During the 1950's a 'potato head' meant a stupid, oafish person.

According to the US Department of Agriculture, survival is possible on a diet consisting solely of potatoes and whole milk.

 OTATOES PAPRIKASH

(HUNGARY)

Serves 4

15 g (½ oz) unsalted butter

1 medium onion, finely chopped

1 medium green pepper, cored, seeded and coarsely chopped

1 medium yellow pepper, cored, seeded and coarsely chopped

4 medium firm-fleshed potatoes, peeled and cut crossways into 3 mm (⅛ in) thick slices, preferably using a food processor fitted with a slicing disc or a mandoline. (Note: The slice should be thin enough to see the outline of the knife through it.)

1 ripe medium tomato, peeled, seeded and coarsely chopped

250 ml (8 fl oz) home-made chicken stock

1 tablespoon plus 2 teaspoons sweet Hungarian paprika (Source List, page 142)

1½ teaspoons caraway seeds

Pinch cayenne pepper

Salt and freshly ground pepper to taste

4 tablespoons soured cream or plain low-fat yogurt, at room temperature, to garnish

Finely chopped fresh parsley, preferably Italian flat-leaf, to garnish

1. In a large heavy frying pan over medium high heat, melt the butter. Add the onion and peppers and cook, stirring often, for 6 minutes or just until the peppers are tender.

2. Stir in the potatoes, tomato, chicken stock, paprika, caraway seeds and cayenne pepper. Bring to the boil, then reduce the heat to low and partially cover. Simmer, stirring occasionally, for 10 to 15 minutes or until the potatoes are soft but not falling apart. Season to taste with salt and pepper. (The recipe can be made up to this point 1 day ahead. Cool, cover and refrigerate. Combine with 125 ml (4 fl oz) water and reheat gently over very low heat before proceeding with recipe.)

3. Divide among 4 shallow bowls. Garnish each with a dollop of soured cream, sprinkle with parsley and serve.

POTATO POTPOURRI

★ On August 25, 1988 Peter Dowdeswell of Earls Barton set the record for eating 1.3 kg (3 lb) of potatoes in 1 minute 22 seconds.

★ In February, 1977, Charles Chip, Inc., of Mountville, Pennsylvania produced the largest crisps ever from oversized potatoes. They were 10 × 17.5 cm (4 × 7 in).

★ The largest potato was reported on February 17, 1795 from Thomas Seddal's garden in Chester. It weighed 8.2 kg (18¼ lb).

★ On October 18, 1982, Ovid Harrison of Kite, Georgia, produced the largest sweet potato. It weighed 18 kg (40¾ lb).

GAME CHIPS OR CRISPS

(BRITAIN)

Serves 4

*2 litres (3½ pints) sunflower,
  groundnut or corn oil, for
  deep frying*
*4 medium baking potatoes,
  peeled and cut crossways into
  slices 3 mm (⅛ in) thick with
  a food processor fitted with a
  slicing blade or a mandoline
  (Or cut into 3 mm/⅛ in thick
  waffled slices, using the
  mandoline.)*
120 g (4 oz) cornflour
Salt to taste (optional)

1. In a very large heavy-based pan or deep fryer over medium high heat, heat the oil until it reaches 185°C (365°F) on a deep-fat thermometer. To test, drop a potato slice into the oil. If it sizzles, the oil is hot enough.

2. Meanwhile, put the potato slices in a colander and rinse under cold running water. Drain and pat dry while rubbing with kitchen paper to help remove some of the surface starch. In a large bowl put the cornflour and the potato slices and toss together until the slices are evenly coated, shaking off any excess cornflour.

3. When the oil is ready, lower an empty deep-frying basket into the oil to coat. (*Note*: Be careful—wear oven gloves when deep frying.) Then lift it out of the oil and add a batch of potato slices to the oiled basket. Be careful not to crowd the basket. Lower the basket back into the oil. Deep fry the potato slices for about 3 minutes or until crisp and lightly golden brown. (*Note*: Be careful not to overcook the crisps, as they will continue to cook slightly even after you remove them.) Lift the basket out, holding it over the pan to drain, then empty the basket on to a baking sheet lined with kitchen paper to drain. Transfer the crisps to a baking dish and place in a preheated low oven to keep warm.

4. Repeat with the remaining potatoes, transferring them to the warm oven in between batches to keep warm.

5. Just before serving, if liked sprinkle the crisps lightly with salt. Do not salt until just before serving because salt breaks down the oil. Serve hot.

CARAMELISED POTATOES

100 g (3½ oz) caster sugar
30 g (1 oz) unsalted butter,
   melted
1 tablespoon sunflower or
   vegetable oil
16 small new potatoes, scraped,
   steamed just until tender
   (page 136) and patted dry
Freshly ground pepper to taste

(DENMARK)

Serves 4

Place the sugar in a large heavy frying pan over medium low heat. Cook, stirring often with a wooden spoon, for about 5 to 8 minutes or until the sugar melts and comes to the boil. Boil (do not stir) for about 2 to 4 minutes or until the mixture turns golden brown but is still syrupy. Do not allow the caramel to overcook or it will be bitter. Working quickly, stir in the melted butter and oil until well blended. Then stir in the cooked potatoes, shaking the pan constantly to rotate the potatoes until they are evenly coated with the caramel. Season with pepper and serve at once. Caramelised potatoes complement a main course of roast lamb or turkey.

POTATO POTPOURRI

According to the 1990 *Guinness Book of World Records*, in May 1969, Paul G Tully of Brisbane University, Australia, set the record for crisp consumption. He ate 30 (60 g / 2 oz) bags in 24 minutes 33.6 seconds, without a drink.

It takes 5 tonnes of raw potatoes to make 1 tonne of crisps.

POTATO POTPOURRI

Among the old-fashioned (but still popular) foodstuffs made with potatoes are: potato flour, potato starch and even potato syrup! Potato syrup was a familiar product in Victorian times: it is very sweet and can be used in place of honey in recipes.

CHILLIED BATTER–FRIED SHOESTRING POTATOES

3 litres (5 pints) sunflower,
   groundnut or corn oil, for
   deep frying
3 medium baking potatoes,
   peeled and cut lengthways
   into julienne strips (as thick
   as a matchstick), made as
   long as possible to resemble
   shoestrings, by using a
   mandoline or a food processor
   fitted with a shredding blade,
   or a rotary grater with large-
   holed drum
2 size-3 eggs, lightly beaten
2 tablespoons skimmed or whole
   milk
2 to 3 fresh green chillies,
   seeded, ribs removed and very
   finely chopped (page 59)
250 g (9 oz) cornmeal
3 tablespoons mild chilli powder
Salt to taste (optional)

Tomato ketchup, to serve
   (optional)

(MEXICO)

Serves 4

1. In a very large heavy pan or deep fryer over medium high heat, heat the oil until it reaches 190°C (375°F) on a deep-fat thermometer. To test, drop a potato shoestring into the oil. If it sizzles the oil is hot enough.

2. Meanwhile, in a large bowl combine the eggs and milk and whisk until well blended. Add the shoestrings and gently stir until well coated. Drain in a colander. Then toss together with the chopped chillies until well coated. In another large bowl combine the cornmeal and chilli powder. Stir until well blended. Add the shoestrings to the cornmeal mixture and toss until evenly coated. Shake off any excess.

3. When the oil is ready, lower an empty deep-frying basket into the oil to coat. (*Note*: Be careful—wear oven gloves when deep frying.) Then lift it out of the oil and add a batch of shoestrings to the oiled basket. Be careful not to crowd the basket. Lower the basket back into the oil. Deep fry the shoestrings for 2 or 3 minutes or until crisp and lightly golden brown. (*Note*: Be careful not to overcook the shoestrings as they will continue to cook slightly even after you remove them.) Lift the basket out, holding it over the pan to drain, then empty the basket on to a baking sheet lined with kitchen paper to drain briefly. Transfer the potatoes to a baking dish and place in a preheated low oven to keep warm until ready to serve.

4. Repeat with the remaining batter-coated shoestrings, skimming the surface of the oil in between batches to keep it clean, draining and transferring each batch to the oven to keep warm until ready to serve.

5. Just before serving, sprinkle the shoestrings with salt if liked. Do not salt until just before serving because salt breaks down the oil. Serve hot, with tomato ketchup if desired, for guests to help themselves.

4 medium baking potatoes,
  thoroughly washed
Sunflower or vegetable oil, to
  grease
60 g (2 oz) unsalted butter,
  melted
1 teaspoon coarse sea salt
1 tablespoon dried breadcrumbs
½ teaspoon paprika, preferably
  Hungarian semisweet or hot
  (Source Lists, page 142), to
  garnish

> "Forget caviar and
> candy for once, why
> not give potatoes for
> Christmas?"
> —Lynda Brown, The
> Guardian, 1987

(SWEDEN)

Serves 4

ASSELBACK POTATOES

(Roasted Potatoes)

1. Preheat the oven to 230°C (450°F or gas 8).

2. Peel the potatoes and place them in a bowl of cold water, making sure they are completely immersed to help prevent discoloration while cutting them. Place a potato in the hollow of a deep wooden spoon, large enough to hold the potato firmly so it can be sliced. Beginning 1 cm (½ in) from the end of the potato, carefully make 3 mm (⅛ in) thick slices down the length of the potato just until the knife stops at the rim of the spoon (do not cut all the way through the potato) ending 1 cm (½ in) from the opposite end. Repeat with the remaining potatoes.

3. Drain. Pat dry the potatoes with kitchen paper. Grease the bottom of a 23 cm (9 in) square baking dish (large enough to hold the potatoes in a single layer) with a little oil. Transfer the potatoes to the dish cut side up. Brush the entire surface of each potato with 1½ teaspoons of the melted butter (a total of 30 g/1 oz) and sprinkle the tops with the sea salt.

4. Roast the potatoes for 40 to 50 minutes or until the potatoes are golden brown and tender when pierced with a fork. Remove the baking dish from the oven. Sprinkle each potato with the breadcrumbs and drizzle with the remaining melted butter (1½ teaspoons per potato). Return the baking dish to the oven and roast for 5 minutes more. Sprinkle the paprika in a strip down the centre of each potato and serve at once. Hasselback Potatoes complement a pork, fish, chicken, beef or lamb dish.

 ECRET INGREDIENT COOKIES

(UNITED STATES)
Makes 24 biscuits

175 g (6 oz) plain flour
¼ teaspoon salt
1¼ teaspoons baking powder
120 g (4 oz) unsalted butter,
   melted
150 g (5 oz) caster sugar
1 size-3 egg, lightly beaten
1 teaspoon vanilla essence
¼ teaspoon ground cinnamon
30 g (1 oz) unsalted potato
   crisps, crushed
60 g (2 oz) shelled pecan nut
   halves, to decorate (optional)

1. Sift together the flour, salt and baking powder three times. In a medium bowl mix together the melted butter and sugar until well blended. Beat in the egg, vanilla essence and cinnamon until well blended.

2. Gradually add the flour mixture to the egg mixture, beating well after each addition. Stir in the potato crisps until well blended.

3. Shape the mixture into a roll about 17.5 cm (7 in) long and 5 cm (2 in) in diameter. Wrap the dough roll in greaseproof paper, sealing the ends tightly. (The recipe can be made up to this point 3 days ahead. Wrap and refrigerate.) Chill in the refrigerator overnight or place in the freezer just until firm and it can be easily sliced.

4. Preheat the oven to 180°C (350°F or gas 4).

5. Unwrap the dough and cut the roll into 5 mm (¼ in) thick slices. Arrange on an ungreased baking sheet 2.5 cm (1 in) apart. Place a pecan nut half in the centre of each biscuit if using. Bake for 12 to 15 minutes or until the edges are very lightly browned. Serve warm, or transfer to a rack to cool and serve at room temperature. Store in an airtight container or jar for up to 4 days.

★ POTATO FUN AND GAMES ★

★ Potato stamp printing. Cut a potato in half lengthways and using a pen draw a design such as a tree or flower on the cut side of the spud. Using a small sharp knife cut straight down to the depth of 1 cm (½ in), tracing the design. Then, holding the knife horizontally, very carefully cut round the design only to the depth of the 1 cm (½ in) mark. Using a paint brush lightly paint the colour(s) of your choice on the design, then press the potato stamp to print the design. You can print on paper, cloth, or wood.

★ 'HOT POTATO' The players sit down and join hands, forming a circle. A designated 'potato caller' is outside the circle, facing the opposite direction. A 'hot potato' (replaced by a bean bag) is quickly passed from one player to another, until the caller yells 'Hot Potato!' The player holding the potato at this time joins the potato caller and they form a circle of their own. The callers choose a number, count to it in a whisper and then yell 'Hot Potato!' The player with the potato in his hands at that time joins the caller circle. The game continues until the last player moves to the potato callers circle.

★ SPUD SLANG ★

Spud

Lumper

Tater

Earth Apple

Irish Grape

Lunker (large potato)

BLUE RIBBON SWEET POTATO DOUGHNUTS

(UNITED STATES)

*Makes about
30 small doughnuts
and holes*

2 size-3 eggs

120 g (4 oz) light soft brown
sugar

250 g (9 oz) mashed yellow or
orange fleshed sweet potatoes
(page 133)

250 ml (8 fl oz) buttermilk

45 g (1½ oz) unsalted butter,
melted

½ teaspoon freshly ground
pepper

½ teaspoon ground mace

500 g (1 lb 2 oz) plain flour,
plus more to dust

1 tablespoon baking powder

½ teaspoon bicarbonate of soda

¾ teaspoon salt

3 litres (5 pints) sunflower or
vegetable oil, for frying

4 tablespoons caster sugar
mixed with 1 tablespoon
ground cinnamon, to garnish
(optional)

124

1. In a medium bowl beat together the eggs, brown sugar, mashed sweet potatoes, buttermilk, melted butter, pepper and mace until well blended.

2. In a separate medium bowl sift together 425 g (15 oz) of the flour, the baking powder, bicarbonate of soda and salt.

3. Stir enough of the flour mixture into the egg mixture just until the mixture forms a soft dough, reserving the remainder. Turn out on to a lightly floured work surface and knead for 10 turns, working in the remaining flour mixture until the dough is less sticky and is manageable. Pat or roll out the dough to a uniform 1 cm (½ in) thickness. Cut the dough with a well-floured 6 cm (2½ in) doughnut cutter. (Or use 2 different-sized biscuit cutters. One should be about 6 cm (2½ in) in diameter, the other 2.5 cm (1 in) for the doughnut hole.) Dip the cutter back into the flour between cuts. Re-roll scraps of dough and repeat the process until you have about 30 doughnuts and holes. Allow the doughnuts and holes to stand for 10 minutes.

4. Meanwhile, in a very large heavy pan or deep fryer heat the oil until a deep-fat thermometer registers 180°C (350°F).

5. Using an oiled fish slice, add a batch of 6 to 8 doughnuts (do not crowd the pan), sliding them gently one at a time into the oil. After the doughnuts rise to the surface, fry them for 2 or 3 minutes on each side. Use long-handled tongs to turn them over so that both sides brown evenly. Transfer to kitchen paper to drain, and repeat the process with the remaining doughnuts. Repeat the process with the doughnut holes in batches of 10 to 12. After the holes rise to the surface fry them for about 1 minute, rotating them gently so they brown evenly. Transfer them to kitchen paper to drain. Using a fine-mesh sieve lightly dust the hot doughnuts and holes with the cinnamon and sugar mixture if using and serve at once.

Sauce:

Makes 250 ml (8 fl oz)

175 ml (6 fl oz) rice wine vinegar

60 ml (2 fl oz) soy sauce

2 teaspoons grated peeled fresh root ginger

1 teaspoon freshly grated orange or lemon zest

2 cloves garlic, crushed

Tempura:

3 litres (5½ pints) groundnut, sunflower or corn oil, for deep frying

¼ teaspoon Oriental sesame oil (optional)

2 size-3 egg yolks, lightly beaten

250 ml (8 fl oz) iced water

120 g (4 oz) plain flour, plus 60 g (2 oz) to dust

½ teaspoon baking powder

½ teaspoon salt

2 medium yellow or orange fleshed sweet potatoes, boiled until just tender (page 136), peeled and cut into 3 mm (⅛ in) thick slices

4 sprigs fresh parsley, preferably Italian flat-leaf, dried well, to garnish (optional)

1. To prepare the sauce: in a heavy non-reactive saucepan over very low heat, combine the rice wine vinegar, soy sauce, ginger, orange zest and garlic. Heat gently, stirring occasionally, until ready to serve.

2. To prepare the tempura: in a large heavy pan or deep fryer over medium high heat, heat the groundnut oil with the sesame oil if used until it reaches 180°C (360°F) on a deep-fat thermometer. To test, drop a little batter into the oil. If it sinks and then rises to the surface, the oil is hot enough.

3. Meanwhile, in a medium bowl combine the egg yolks, iced water, 120 g (4 oz) flour, the baking powder and salt. Stir, do not whisk, until just blended (the batter will still be lumpy). Pat dry the sweet potato slices to remove excess moisture. Put the 60 g (2 oz) flour in another medium bowl and add the sweet potato slices, tossing together until the slices are evenly coated and shaking off any excess flour.

4. When the oil is ready, with tongs or chopsticks dip a few of the sweet potato slices into the batter until evenly coated and using a long-handled wire skimmer or slotted spoon drop the sweet potatoes, one by one, in small batches (do not crowd the pan—the slices should not touch each other)

SWEET POTATO TEMPURA WITH DIPPING SAUCE

(JAPAN)

Serves 4

into the hot oil. (*Note*: Be careful—wear oven gloves when deep frying.) Deep fry the sweet potatoes for 1 to 2 minutes or until the edges are light golden brown, then flip over and deep fry the other side for about 1 to 2 minutes more or until puffed, crisp and light golden brown. (*Note*: Be careful not to overcook the tempura as it will continue to cook slightly even after you remove it.) Transfer the potatoes to a baking sheet lined with kitchen paper to drain briefly, then to a heated platter to keep warm in between batches.

5. Repeat with the remaining potatoes and batter, skimming the surface of the oil often in between batches to keep it clean, and then draining and transferring each batch of tempura to the platter to keep warm until ready to serve.

6. Just before serving, if liked deep fry the parsley sprigs (do not dip in batter) for about 2 seconds, turning often, just until crisp (not browned). Drain briefly on the kitchen paper until ready to serve.

7. To serve, divide the tempura among 4 plates. Garnish each with a fried parsley sprig and accompany with a bowl of hot dipping sauce. Serve at once. Serve as a first course or as a side dish.

POTATO POTPOURRI

The potato tuber is the only edible part of the potato plant. The rest, including the flower, is inedible. The potato sprout when eaten in large quantities can be toxic. ★ Potatoes can help reduce air pollution since they produce ethanol. ★ Scientists at the Argonne National Laboratory in the state of Illinois are developing a process to convert potato starch from potato peelings into bio- and photodegradable plastics.

4 tablespoons usli ghee *(page 106) or sunflower oil, plus more if needed*

10 small new potatoes, scraped, pricked all over with a fork, and quartered; if large cut into eighths so all pieces are uniform in size, or use a melon baller to scoop the flesh from 4 large firm-fleshed potatoes into small balls

225 g (8 oz) onion, finely chopped

1 tablespoon grated peeled fresh root ginger

Seeds from 4 cardamom pods, preferably green

½ teaspoon turmeric powder

½ teaspoon cayenne pepper

2 teaspoons ground coriander

1 teaspoon ground cinnamon

½ teaspoon ground cloves

2 tablespoons fresh lemon juice

½ cup plain low-fat yogurt, at room temperature

½ cup freshly grated coconut or unsweetened desiccated coconut, finely chopped

1 teaspoon salt

½ teaspoon freshly ground pepper

DUM ALOO

1. In a large heavy frying pan or very large saucepan (large enough to hold the potatoes in a single layer) over medium high heat, heat 3 tablespoons of the *usli ghee*. Add the potatoes and sauté them, adding more *usli ghee* if needed to coat the pan, for 12 to 15 minutes, or until they are well browned and tender when pierced with a fork. Using a slotted spoon, transfer to a bowl and reserve.

2. Add the remaining 2 tablespoons *usli ghee* to the pan with the onion. Sauté the onion for 5 to 7 minutes, or until golden brown.

(INDIA)

Serves 4

*(Potatoes in Spicy
Yogurt Sauce)*

3. Reduce the heat to medium and add the ginger, cardamom seeds, turmeric, cayenne pepper, ground coriander, cinnamon, cloves and lemon juice, stirring vigorously for 10 seconds. Reduce the heat to low and stir in the yogurt, coconut, salt and pepper until well blended. Bring to the boil. Add the reserved potatoes and cook for 5 minutes, stirring often. (*Note*: If the sauce is too thick, stir in a few tablespoons of water until desired consistency is reached.) Serve at once. (This recipe is best when made at least 4 hours in advance or up to 2 days ahead. Allow to cool, cover and refrigerate. Reheat over low heat before serving.)

A Note to the Health-Conscious Reader

My goal has been to create recipes featuring the potato that are healthful and that are conservative with the use of fat, sugar and salt without forsaking flavour. I have not completely avoided ingredients such as butter, milk, eggs, sugar and salt since in many instances these are necessary to maintain the integrity and particular flavour of a traditional ethnic recipe. I have, however, reduced the amount of less healthful ingredients, making the collection of recipes more 'health-wise'.

Here are simple ways in which you can make recipes more healthy:

★ Use whole milk in place of beaten egg for glazes on pastry, breads, etc.

★ Rinse and drain oil-packed or brine-packed foods like anchovies, beans, olives and capers before using.

★ Trim meats and poultry of excess fat.

★ Whenever possible, keep vegetable and fruit skins intact, because this is where most of the nutrients are.

★ Use non-stick pans. It allows you to use less fat in cooking; in some cases, none at all, as with an omelet. Another bonus is that non-stick pans are easier to wash!

★ When shopping, read all labels carefully. Nutritionally 'modified' products are not always what they seem. For example, 'light' may actually refer to the taste or consistency of a product. Claims can be ambiguous — calories and fat content might be the same! Also, make sure that after being modified the product is still nutritious!

★ In many of the recipes I have included page references that will answer any questions you might have.

They may direct you to a quick cooking method, such as for boiling potatoes, or to a concise summary of the differences amongst potato types, such as the confusion between yams and sweet potatoes. More important than this distinction is to understand that different varieties of potato lend themselves to different cooking methods. Knowing which type of potato to use is essential to well-prepared dishes. In other cases the reference is to a tip on the preparation of an ingredient — how to grate fresh coconut or seed a chilli.

Potato Preliminaries

Even though there are many varieties of white potatoes (over 200 grown in Britain), it is unlikely that you will find more than 15 throughout the year at your green-grocer or supermarket. If you want to try more unusual varieties — purple-fleshed, yellow-fleshed and the like — try delicatessens and specialist greengrocers, or even mail-order sources.

Potatoes are categorised as either early or maincrop. Earlies come on the market at the end of May, with so-called second earlies at the beginning of August. Maincrop potatoes appear in mid-September and are available until the end of May. This long season of availability should keep your pantry well stocked year round. Even within these major categories, however, there are numerous varieties from which to choose. Experiment with each type to recognise differences in flavour and learn which types harmonise best with specific foods.

Some common earlies are Jersey Royal, Maris Bard, Maris Peer, Pentland Javelin and Ulster Sceptre; second earlies include Estima and Wilja. The maincrop potatoes most commonly available are Cara, Desiree, King Edward, Maris Piper, Pentland Crown, Pentland Squire and Romano.

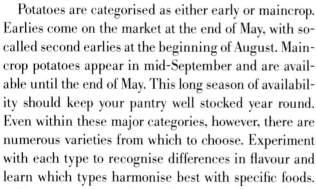

BASIC TYPES

Both earlies and maincrop may be either 'waxy' and firm-fleshed or 'floury' — or both. Waxy potatoes are lower in starch and have a waxy, moist interior. Potatoes described as 'floury' are high in starch and have a drier mealy or floury interior. These terms are useful for determining how to prepare potatoes. How a potato cooks depends upon its starch content. For example, waxy potatoes contain more liquid; they keep their shape, therefore, when cooked and do not absorb as much liquid when added to a soup or salad. They work best, in fact, when used in these ways. Floury potatoes are great for such classic yet simple preparation methods as mashed or baked potatoes because they have a fluffier texture when cooked.

Choosing the right variety of potato to use in a dish is very important. Waxy, firm-fleshed potatoes are good for cooking techniques where the potatoes need to hold their shape, such as boiling, steaming, roasting and sautéeing. Floury potatoes are good for cooking techniques where it doesn't matter if the potato keeps its shape, such as baking, mashing (or for mashed potatoes to be used as an ingredient in baked goods), puréeing and deep frying.

The following list will guide you when choosing a potato for a recipe:

★ boiling: earlies such as Jersey Royal, Estima, Maris Bard, Pentland Javelin and Wilja; maincrop such as Desiree.

★ mashing: maincrop such as King Edward, Maris Piper and Romano.

★ baking: maincrop such as Cara, Desiree, Maris Piper, Pentland Crown, Pentland Squire and Romano.

★ roasting and for chips: maincrop such as Desiree, King Edward, Maris Piper and Pentland Dell; earlies such as Ulster Sceptre.

TATER TEST

If you have a hard time deciding whether a potato is waxy or floury, use the following test, based on Harold McGee's *On Food and Cooking*, to establish type.

Make a solution of 2 parts water to 1 part salt. Add the potato. If it is waxy it will float; if floury it will sink.

KNOWING THE NEW POTATO

New potatoes are not a separate kind of potato, but rather any freshly dug potato that has not reached maturity. Size, variety and type (waxy or floury) are irrelevant. True new potatoes are sold from late winter or early spring through midsummer. Everyone prefers the smallest ones possible, as they are slightly sweet (not all the sugar has turned to starch yet). They are a gastronomic treat, not to be missed! A new potato hasn't fully developed its skin yet either, so if you are unsure whether or not it is a freshly dug potato, just rub it with your thumb. If the skin is thin and flakes easily, it is most certainly a new potato.

When preparing new potatoes, don't scrub them, just gently wipe the delicate skin clean with damp kitchen paper before cooking. They are also quite perishable, so use them quickly. Since their flesh is moist and waxy, they are at their very best unpeeled and roasted, steamed or boiled.

SWEET POTATOES VERSUS YAM

Even though the sweet potato can be substituted for the potato in any recipe, technically speaking the sweet potato is *not* an actual potato. The sweet potato (*Ipomoea batata*) is a member of the morning glory family, whereas the potato (*Solanum tuberosum*) belongs to the nightshade family.

133

The sweet potato has varieties whose skin ranges from pinkish to reddish brown in colour and flesh yellowish white to a rich, deep orange — making them appropriate ingredient choices for autumn and winter meals. Most of the recipes in this book that call for sweet potatoes ask for the yellow or orange-fleshed variety. This is done to distinguish them from the yam, with which they are often confused, even by greengrocers and supermarkets.

Sweet potatoes are not related to the true yam (*Dioscorea bulbifera*), which grows on a tropical climbing vine. If you want to try a genuine yam, look for it in a market or shop that specializes in Caribbean food. Gourmet shops and mail-order sources may also seasonally carry true yams, so you might also explore these possibilities. Whether you use the sweet potato or the true yam for the recipes in this book, you are bound to be delighted by their interesting and delightful tastes.

THE POTATO BIN

Before embarking on the recipes in this book, it's a good idea to familiarise yourself with general preparation and cooking methods that are used for both potatoes and sweet potatoes.

SELECTING SPUDS   Peeled and/or cut potatoes discolour (darken) when exposed to the air. Although this isn't harmful, it is unsightly and is easily avoided. When peeling or cutting potatoes, have a bowl of cold water to hand. As you work add the potatoes to the bowl of water, making sure they are completely immersed. When ready to proceed with the recipe, drain the potatoes well and blot them dry with kitchen paper to remove the surface starch and to prevent splattering when cooking in fat.

Avoid green-tinged white potatoes altogether; green spots or green-tinged flesh are an indication of solanine, which in small quantities can make you feel ill — in large doses it is poisonous. Exposure to strong light causes potato flesh to turn green so store potatoes in a dark place. Don't try to cut the green flesh away, simply discard the entire potato.

The 'eyes' of a potato each have a bud underneath, from which a sprout grows into a mature plant. If a potato has sprouted, throw it away. Don't bother to cut away the sprouts because the potato won't be tasty anyway. Also, sprouts on a potato, when eaten in quantity, can be harmful.

Cooking the Perfect Potato

YIELD Naturally the recipe you use will state the number of servings. However, if you have been inspired to create your own recipes and are ad-libbing, here are some guidelines to help you to estimate the yield of potatoes and sweet potatoes:

1 medium potato or 1 small sweet potato = 1 serving
4 small new potatoes = 1 serving
6 very small new potatoes = 1 serving

BOILING

1. Use only a variety of potato suitable for boiling (page 132), unless making mashed potatoes, in which case use a baking variety of potato (page 132). Gently scrub whole potatoes under cold running water until clean and don't peel them before boiling. The potato skin is a natural envelope that seals in flavour and moisture. (The skin is also very nutritious.) In a heavy-based pan over medium heat, put the potatoes, cover with cold water by about 5 cm (2 in) and bring to the boil. You can add 1 teaspoon of salt to each litre (1¾ pints) of water before bringing to the boil, but this is optional. Then reduce the heat and simmer, partly covered, for 15–25 minutes, depending on potato size and quantity.

2. If boiling new potatoes, immerse them in already boiling water and follow the directions above, but cook for only 10–15 minutes, again depending on the size of the potatoes and quantity in the pan. (*Note*: It is also a nice touch to boil potatoes in home-made stock.)

3. When the potatoes are tender — pierce the thickest one in the centre with a fork — drain them in a colander at once. If the potatoes are to be used in a salad, refresh them under cold running water and proceed with the recipe. If they are to be served warm, cover gently with a clean tea towel to keep warm until ready to serve or proceed with the recipe. If you are going to peel and/or mash the potatoes, this is easiest to do if the potatoes are warm. Just allow them to cool enough so that they can be handled.

STEAMING

Because of their waxy texture, it is preferable only to steam potatoes suitable for boiling (page 132). Gently scrub the potatoes under cold running water and place unpeeled or peeled potatoes directly on a rack or in a steamer basket in a heavy pan over 5 cm (2 in) of boiling water (the water level should not touch the bottom of the rack or basket). Cover the pan and steam the potatoes for 15–30 minutes, depending on the size of the potatoes and quantity in the pan. Steaming times will be longer than those for boiling. Also, you may have to add a little more boiling water halfway through the cooking process. Proceed with step 3 as directed above.

AROMATIC STEAMING LIQUID To make your potatoes really special, add aromatic seasonings such as garlic, fresh or dried herbs, spices — allspice or juniper berries, cinnamon sticks or peppercorns — fresh root ginger, citrus peels and so on to the steaming water. The vapour will impart a subtle flavour to the potatoes. I have also experimented with fresh vegetable or fruit juices. Home-made vegetable or seafood stock works wonderfully, as does wine or other liquor-spiked liquid. Be creative and taste the marvelous results.

BAKING

1. Use only a variety of potato suitable for baking (page 132) unless otherwise directed in a recipe. Preheat the oven to 230°C (450°F or gas 8). Gently scrub the potato clean under cold running water and then pat dry with kitchen paper (do not peel). Using a skewer or fine-pronged fork, pierce the potato in several places. Bake the potato directly on the oven rack for 35–45 minutes (depending on the size of the potato and if it is sharing the oven with other dishes), or until the middle of the thickest potato feels soft when squeezed (through an oven glove!) with your fingers. If you can, bake only 4 to 6 medium potatoes per oven rack. Also, try not to place the potatoes close to one another or other dishes as this will reduce the crispness of the skin. (*Note*: The longer

you bake the potato the better. If you like a very crisp skin and fluffy centre, bake up to 1¼ hours, sometimes even longer, depending on desired texture of the skin.) Don't wrap the potato in foil or the skin will be soggy and the potato mushy in texture. If you want a soft skin, instead of a crisp skin, then rub the potato with a little butter or oil before baking.

I don't recommend using the microwave oven for 'baking' a potato as it really steams it, resulting in a soggy skin. If time is not a factor and your reason for using the microwave to bake a potato is simply that you don't want to heat up a large oven, then I recommend a toaster oven rather than a microwave.

TOPPINGS Baked potatoes are the prize, the benchmark of potato cookery. A baked potato with an appropriate topping can be an entire meal! It is fun to create themes with potato toppings, such as Cowboy-Style (*chili con carne* with grated Cheddar cheese) or Chinese-Style (your favourite meat or vegetable stir-fry, garnished with crunchy deep-fried noodles). Always try to use low-fat, reduced calorie and low-sodium staples, such as low-fat cottage cheese and low-fat plain yogurt, to make this delicious treat more wholesome.

ROASTING

1. To roast is to bake in an uncovered tin with dry heat, producing a crisp, dark exterior and a moist interior. Roasting works especially well with small unpeeled new potatoes or larger unpeeled boiling potatoes that can be quartered, sliced, or cut into large cubes. Preheat the oven to 190°C (375°F or gas 5). Gently scrub the potatoes under cold running water and pat dry with kitchen paper, or wash and cut large potatoes accordingly. Transfer the potatoes to a roasting tin (large

enough to hold the potatoes in a single layer) and coat lightly with olive oil or vegetable oil or dot with butter. Add your favourite seasonings to taste — fresh or dried herbs (rosemary is always a favourite) or peeled garlic cloves — or place the potatoes on a bed of thinly sliced onions sprinkled with paprika. Salt and freshly ground pepper are welcome. Roast, tossing occasionally to baste with oil, for 35–45 minutes, or until the potatoes are tender when the thickest one is pierced in the centre with a fork. Serve hot.

MASHING

1. This is not really a cooking method, as the potatoes have already been boiled or steamed. Use a variety of potato suitable for mashing (page 132); they make a fluffier-textured mashed potato. I don't recommend baking or roasting the potatoes (the dry-heat cooking method) before mashing as the texture of the final dish of mashed potatoes is not as smooth. However, if the mashed potatoes are to be used as an ingredient in cakes or breads, it is preferable to bake the potatoes first, rather than boil or steam them. The lower water content makes for a better-textured bread, cake or biscuit.

2. To mash, I suggest an old-fashioned potato masher or large fork. Mash the warm peeled potatoes in up-and-down movements to incorporate as much air as possible and to give a lighter consistency, not a sideways or circular movement. The motion is very important. (Please don't use a food processor, blender or electric mixer to mash — the result will be glue.) Use a fork or spoon to blend in your choice of embellishments to enrich the mashed potatoes. Serve at once or, if you must, keep warm, partly covered, in a heatproof bowl or in the top of a double boiler set over warm (not simmering or boiling) water.

SAUTÉING AND SHALLOW AND DEEP FRYING

—Always blot potatoes dry with kitchen paper before sautéing or frying to prevent them from splattering in the hot fat. They will still make a 'sputter' noise, but should not make the oil actually splatter.

—When sautéing or shallow frying, heat the pan first, then add the oil. The rule is: add cold oil to a hot pan.

—When sautéing or frying do not crowd the pan. Cook the food in batches and always cut it into uniform pieces.

—When frying protect yourself from burns with flameproof oven gloves or long-handled tongs.

—For frying, avoid oils sold as 'vegetable oils'. I suggest using sunflower oil, because it stands up well to high temperatures. However, if you want flavour, use corn or groundnut oil.

—Do not use oil with an altered scent or taste. This usually indicates that it has become rancid.

TO AVOID POTENTIALLY DANGEROUS SPLATTERING

For shallow frying, add oil to a depth of about 5 mm (¼ in) depending on the recipe instructions, but make sure the pan isn't more than one quarter full. When adding oil for deep frying, add enough to immerse the food, but don't fill the pan more than half full.

—For shallow frying, use a wide shallow heavy pan. For deep frying, use a heavy pan, deeper than it is wide.

—I don't recommend re-using oils after frying because the smoking point will be lower each time it is used and the flavour is never as good. If thriftiness is your motive, choose a less expensive oil.

GRILLING OVER COALS

Try barbecuing potatoes instead of baking them. Lightly coat the unpeeled potatoes with oil, and place on the barbecue grid. Grill over medium-hot coals, with the barbecue lid closed, rotating the potatoes occasionally, for 45–60 minutes (depending on the size of the potatoes and the quantity of food on the barbecue).

Or, if you want barbecued sliced potatoes, parboil peeled potatoes until just tender. Cut them crossways into 1 cm (½ in) thick slices, lightly coat with oil and barbecue for about 3 minutes per side, just to heat through and achieve grill marks for an attractive presentation.

Some other ideas: Shish-Kebabs: parboil unpeeled whole new potatoes until tender, lightly rub with oil, thread on to skewers and proceed with a kebab recipe. Try barbecuing potato skins for a snack: use scooped-out potato skins left-over from making mashed potatoes. Fold each skin in half lengthways, lightly coat with oil and place on barbecue grid. Grill, flipping once, until the skins are crispy. Don't forget that you can use aromatic wood chips such as hickory, mesquite and apple wood, or vine cuttings in the fire to add extra flavour to your potatoes.

THE MICROWAVE If you want to preserve the purple flesh of the purple, black or blue variety of potatoes, the microwave oven does a superb job. The microwave is not my personal choice of cooking method. If you want a cooked potato with a soft skin and a moist, creamy texture (as opposed to a cooked potato with a crisp skin and fluffy texture from baking or roasting), then I recommend steaming because it produces a better-textured potato.

If it is a hot day and time is a problem, follow the manufacturer's guidelines for cooking potatoes.

POTATOPHILE SOURCE LISTS

RETAIL STORES FOR POTATOES, KITCHEN TOOLS AND BOOKS

BRIDGE KITCHENWARE
214 East 52nd Street
New York, NY 10022
212-688-4220
Giant selection of cookware, pastry equipment and other specialized kitchen tools.

EL GALINDO, INC.
1601 East 6th Street
Austin, TX 78702
In Texas
512-478-5756
Outside of Texas
800-447-8905
Many types of fresh tortillas and tortilla chips. Also, 30 types of peppers and a generous variety of salsas.

FOOD OF ALL NATIONS
2121 Ivy Road
Charlottesville, VA 22903
804-296-6131
Large selection of international staples and seasonings. They publish a monthly newsletter.

J.B. PRINCE COMPANY
29 West 38th Street
New York, NY 10018
212-302-8611
A showroom located in New York City boasts a very professional selection of international cooking equipment. Several types of man-dolines available. Books geared to the food professional.

HERBS AND SPICES

APHRODISIA PRODUCTS
282 Bleecker Street
New York, NY 10014
212-989-6440
Wide selection of dried herbs and spices. Bulk orders of seasonings available at wholesale prices.

HOUSE OF SPICES
76-17 Broadway
Jackson Heights, NY 11373
718-476-1577
A tremendous selection of Indian and Pakistani utensils, herbs, and foodstuffs.

PAPRIKAS WEISS IMPORTER
1546 Second Avenue
New York, NY 10028
212-288-6117
The *store for Hungarian paprika, available in different strengths. Other Hungarian products and gourmet goods offered.*

SPICE MERCHANT
P.O. Box 524
Jackson Hole, WY 83001
307-733-7811
800-551-5999
Chinese, Japanese, Thai, Indonesian, and Vietnamese seasonings and condiments. Also, Asian food-stuffs and unusual cooking equipment.

MISCELLANEOUS

The Good Potato Guide
(price £1.95 plus postage)
Henry Doubleday Research
Association
Ryton-on-Dunsmore
Coventry CB8 3LG
United Kingdom
Comprehensive information on organically grown varieties available in the UK and elsewhere.

THE POTATO MARKETING BOARD
Broad Field House
4 Between Towns Road
Cowley, Oxford OX4 3NA
United Kingdom
Up-to-date information on potato varieties and seasonal availability.

SEED SAVERS EXCHANGE
R.R. 3, Box 239
Decorah, IA 52101
Members include farmers and serious gardeners dedicated to saving seeds of heirloom vegetables and plants to protect and maintain unusual varieties for future generations.

WORLD FOOD MUSEUM
THE POTATO MUSEUM
P.O. Box 791
Great Falls, VA 22066
The Potato Museum publishes an illustrated newsletter Peelings, just on potatoes, available at a modest fee.

INDEX